Chapter 1 - Introduction

This is:
CHIN KON PAI MEDITATION

By:

Grandmaster
Glenn C. Wilson (2013)

剛軟拳法白龍道

白蓮拳法

Copyright © 2013 by WDWS Publications

All rights reserved. This book or any portion thereof may not be reproduced or used in any manner whatsoever without the express written permission of the publisher.

Printed in the United States of America

First Printing, 2013

ISBN 978-0-9858411-2-6

WDWS Publications

955 W. Lancaster Rd, Suite #1

Orlando, FL 32809

USA

www.pailum.org

Disclaimer

Please note that the author and publisher of this book are NOT RESPONSIBLE in any manner whatsoever for any injury that may result from practicing the techniques and/or following the instruction given within. Since the physical activities described herein may be too strenuous in nature for some readers to engage in safely, it is essential that a physician be consulted prior to training.

Chapter 1 - Introduction

Preface

The journey of one's self through Chin Kon Pai Meditation is a beautiful and fulfilling one. It begins with a desire for truth and peace within. It is not about others, it is about feeding one's self the nourishment of self enlightenment that is achieved through peaceful thought and mind exercise.

Like a flower it will feed on the nourishments of its surrounding nature and ultimately flourish. It will grow and feed on the sunshine that will help in sustaining its fragile life. It will reach out to absorb the nature's life giving element – water. This will nourish and protect the flower as it continues to grow and give beauty to the world around it. If all these factors blend well together the plant will propagate and spread its power to all.

Chin Kon Pai Meditation is the system of mental practice, stimulation, exercise, development and nourishment that feeds our mind. Our minds are the most powerful tool to mankind. We learn to develop a sensitive and powerful source of thought that will aid us for life's peaceful moments and intense challenges.

My teacher taught me the true meaning of self meditation and all of its qualities. The teachings of Chin Kon Pai Meditation were developed and mastered by Dr. Daniel Kalimaahaae Kane Pai and passed on to a few of his chosen students. This form of meditation is practiced through Zen, Chakra and Guided forms of exercise. The influences include, yet are not limited to, a varied list of practices such as Chinese and Tibetan Buddhist techniques, Japanese Zen, India's Vedic and Vipassana teachings, Hawaiian Arts and Native American principles.

For the great honor and opportunity to study and learn this art directly from Dr. Pai I will be forever grateful. I will keep the promise to him that I voiced at our last day together. As we celebrated his birthday, I promised and swore that I will forever keep his dreams and teachings alive. This he asked of me. That was the last time I saw my teacher alive. In his honor I faithfully teach his arts.

Grandmaster – Professor Glenn C. Wilson

Table of Contents

Chapter 1 - Introduction	10
Chapter 2 - Philosophy	22
Chapter 3 - What Is Meditation?	52
Chapter 4 - Elements of Chin Kon Pai Meditation	58
Chapter 5 - Mind, Thought, Action	74
Chapter 6 - Four Supreme States	86
Chapter 7 - Psychology of Meditation	94
Chapter 8 - Find Your Rest	104
Chapter 9 - Chi Development Through Meditation	114
Chapter 10 - Mind Over Matter	120
Chapter 11 - Rest and Motion	128
Chapter 12 - Seven Chakras	136
Chapter 13 - Teenagers and Meditation	148
Chapter 14 - Guided Meditation	154
Chapter 15 - Peace and Joy	164
Chapter 16 - Gallery	172

Chapter 1 - Introduction

Acknowledgements

I find that when authoring any type of writing, it is only accomplished with the great efforts of many people. There is no price that you can put on the passion and hard work that others offer so freely and generously. Such efforts are a testimony to the strength and resolve of our Pai Lum Tao family of martial arts. I thank God and our family every day for being given such a gift.

I would like to acknowledge the following for their tremendous contributions to my writing of this book - Chin Kon Pai Meditation. It has been a pleasure and joy.

- Hilda G. Wilson – contributor and continuous inspiration
- Bryan Naegele – technical expertise, support and photography
- Robert Murphy – contributor
- Carolyn Chen Whately - contributor
- Joe McGuire – contributor
- Conrad Blasko – contributor
- Lance G. Wilson - contributor
- All my students who modeled for the photos
- White Dragon Warrior Society members – support

A special thank you to Simo Denise Vigi, she was the ultimate teacher of Pai Lum Tao internal arts. Her passion for the internal arts of Tai Chi Chuan, Chi Kung and Meditation became a warm light for all of us. Though she has passed on to join her love 'Dr. Daniel Pai', her teachings will endure inside all of us.

I would like to give a special thank you to my direct teacher, 'the late' Great Grandmaster Dr. Daniel Kalimaahaae 'Kane' Pai for the many years of guidance, teachings, patience, support and fatherly love that he gave me. Through my young years as an adolescent Sifu to my years as an experienced master, he was always there for me and led me with his own unique way of doing things. His way was the old way; and he convinced us young students to learn all of the aspects of Pai Lum Tao, internal as well as the external martial aspects. Dr. Pai will always be remembered as one of the foremost teachers of our times and a martial artist, philosopher, teacher, mentor and father figure who feared nothing and learned from everything!

Respectfully,

Professor Glenn C. Wilson - Si Tai Gung Pai Lum Tao

Dedication

I would like to dedicate this book to the following:

My family for their never ending support and patience during all my artistic and writing endeavors. As any author will tell you it takes support from those closest to you to be successful.

My ancestors, a strong blood line beginning with my 'gggggg' grandfather who in the mid 1700s moved from Scotland to the United States and eventually settling in Walker County, Georgia. This very strong lineage of hard working – well educated pioneers set a standard of my present day beliefs and convictions in my fellow man and my God. The blending of blood between the Scottish hunters/farmers and the Native American residents of Georgia created a proud and powerful warrior heart in me that I sincerely respect and recognize.

With honor to my Martial Arts family, Gong Yuen Chuan Fa – Pai Lum Tao. I am blessed as a leader/father of my own family of Chinese / Hawaiian martial arts. I am truly honored to have such wonderful and giving people to train with and share our knowledge together. They desire the internal teachings 'meditation' as much as they long for the external martial arts.

I respect my brothers at the Masonic Lodge in Orlando, Florida that I humbly maintain an honorable membership at. They are always giving and share openly their knowledge and fuel my quest for light. They have helped me in my journey to understand the light of knowledge.

I will always show the greatest admiration and respect to my teacher, (the late) Great Grandmaster – Dr. Daniel Kalimaahaae Pai. He was a true master of Chin Kon Pai Meditation and convinced us young disciples to practice daily. It has been years since his passing and journey to our Lord. His teachings and guidance I will forever hold close to my heart. His teachings will endure for centuries to come.

Chapter 1

Introduction

Chapter 1 - Introduction

There are many types, styles, organizations and theory beliefs to meditation today. What matters most is how it works for you and does it satisfy your need. We all enter our world of meditation practice with our own individual need, desire and preference of practice. If it fits your need, attempt to make it a regular practice that you look forward to doing. It should not become a burden or something you dread partaking in or it will not feed your need and yearning.

Why do we practice Chin Kon Pai, how did it come about and who primarily practices it in today's modern form of practice? Well, we practice Chin Kon Pai meditation for the same reasons most people practice any type or style; that is to relieve stress, minimize our anxiety and try to establish then maintain a healthier way of life. It works well for most people because it is fairly easy to do and the benefits are felt in a relatively fast time for most.

Chin Kon Pai meditation was developed by Chinese/Hawaiian martial arts master Dr. Daniel Kalimaahaae Kane Pai. It is a culmination of a life long endeavor into the Asian arts as well as the ancient and new philosophies of meditation throughout the world. Dr. Pai spent his entire life studying and mastering the Asian Martial Arts as well as philosophies, medicine, herbs and healing. His background in meditation was a thorough as it was varied: he studied the various systems from Tibet, India, China, Japan and even native Hawaiian. He structured a form of meditational exercise that would comprise teachings of Zen, Chakra and Guided Mediations.

When a new student comes to train in Chin Kon Pai they will be evaluated by a certified teacher to help set them on the right path for them. The most important concern when a new student starts is that they understand what they are doing and have a clear vision of where they want their journey to go. After a certified Chin Kon Pai instructor evaluates the new student they are presented with a program that will assure their success and put them on the path to greater peace and joy.

Within the Pai Lum Tao system of Asian / Martial Arts one will be introduced to instructors and elder students will be will to assist them on a regular program. It may be more structured for some and a looser approach for others. The key is that one feels what they are doing is truly for them and becomes a positive part of their everyday life. Lifestyle, food intake, breathing exercises and self understanding are at the center of the Chin Kon Pai vision. It is truly an individual experience that has proven to be a great success for many.

Presently Grandmaster / Professor Glenn C. Wilson carries on the teachings and traditions of Chin Kon Pai Meditation in the 21st century. He was a direct disciple of the legendary Guru / Sijo Dr. Daniel Pai from the mid 1970s until 1993. He received his knowledge and Masters Degree directly from Dr. Pai.

Since Dr. Pai's passing in 1993, Professor Wilson has strived to keep the system and knowledge as pure as possible. He has taught thousands of students throughout the world and continues to keep the fire and energy going for all of those prospective students that hunger for the light of knowledge as well as a healthier and peaceful way of life. Professor Wilson has truly balanced his life with the very art that he teaches others. Keeping one's peace of mind and balance in a stressful society is at the heart of his teaching and life style sharing. I have been his student for more than 18 years. I have attained my Masters Degree in the Pai Lum Tao Asian Arts. This helped put me on my path to achieving a Masters in Science of Oriental Medicine and becoming an Acupuncture Physician. I presently own and operate my own practice Medicinal Life and teach at the Pai Lum Tao Academy in Orlando as well as the Florida College of Integrative Medicine.

Enjoy your journey and embrace your peaceful path.

Robert Murphy AP

Master Pai Lum Tao – Kung Fu, Kenpo, Tai Chi Chuan, Chi Kung & Meditation

Great Grandmaster
Dr. Daniel Kalimaahaae 'Kane' Pai

Great Grandmaster- Pai Lum Tao Martial Arts
Master Level – Chin Kon Pai Meditation
Master Level – Pai Yung Tai Chi
Master Level – Quan Nien Chi Kung
Master Level - Bok Leen Pai Kenpo
10th Level Pai Te Lung Chuan Kung Fu
8th Level Hawaiian Kempo
5th Level Okinawan Kempo
5th Level Aikido
5th Level Jiu Jitsu

Chapter 1 - Introduction

Daniel Kane Pai was born April 4, 1930 in Kameulai Hawaii. He lived the last seventeen years of his life in Florida and passed away in 1993 in the Dominican Republic. Per his request he was laid to rest in his beloved Hawaii. During his sixty-three year journey on earth he built a martial arts legacy throughout North America. Daniel Kalimaahaae Kane Pai did it his way, from the tough streets of Hawaii to forming the largest Kung Fu system in North America during the 60's and 70's. There was no doubt of his command of Pai Lum Tao Martial Arts. He taught a rough/tough type of training, for which the Hawaiian Islands are well known. A young Daniel began training with family members in Hawaii in the disciplines of Kung Fu, Kenpo and Judo-Jujitsu. He would master 'the Pai family' martial arts which contained mainly elements of Dragon and Crane. After the mastery of Dragon, Crane and Tiger, Leopard and Snake were introduced to the young practitioner.

He would balance his rough life and martial arts style with the teachings of meditation, Tai Chi, Chi Kung as well as natural Asian / Hawaiian healing.

His life reflected many changes. He was a teacher of martial arts, a graduate of the Chicago Medical College "Ph.D.", revered master of several forms of meditation, a bodyguard, stunt coordinator, Philosopher and decorated Korean War Veteran. In the seventies, Dr. Pai formed the U.S. White Dragon Martial Arts Society in hopes of standardizing his vast knowledge of martial arts. The students of the sixties and seventies who weathered Pai's rigorous training became known as the "Old School" lineage. Dr. Pai's American team was awarded the Superb Achievement Merit at the Kuoshu event in Taipei in 1976. In 1980 Dr. Pai served as director at the 3rd World Chinese Kuoshu Tournament in Hawaii. During Dr. Pai's visit to Taipei in 1983 he was appointed the United States Vice President of the Worldwide Promotion Association 'Executive Board' of the Kuoshu Federation of the Republic of China. As President of the United States Chinese Kuoshu Federation in 1989 he organized the much-talked about World Chinese Kuoshu tournament in Las Vegas, Nevada.

During the eighties and early nineties Dr. Pai taught a few selected disciples the practice of Chin Kon Pai Meditation. These eager students were chosen for their skill, insight, spirituality and dedication to Pai Lum Tao and their fellow man. Dr. Pai's senior students in meditation were Denise Vigi, Glenn Wilson and Hilda Guerrero Wilson.

In 1990 Dr. Pai and disciple Glenn Wilson began work on forming a structured organization to unite the different factions Pai Lum Tao martial arts, to standardize the curriculum and to legitimize rank. Today this organization is the 'White Dragon Warrior Society'. The Society is 'chaired' by Grand Master Glenn C. Wilson and is dedicated to keeping the dreams of Great Grand Master Daniel Kane Pai alive. Dr. Pai was a true pioneer of Martial Arts, Meditation and Healing Arts in America, a true-life innovator of the modern arts and one of the rare legends in his own time!

Chapter 1 - Introduction

Grandmaster Glenn C. Wilson

'Pai Pao Lung Huit'
'Name given by Great Grandmaster Daniel Kalimaahaae Pai'

5 Times World Champion
8 Times U.S. National Champion
Inducted into 6 Hall of Fames
1984 to 1989 Coach on U.S. National Kung Fu Team
CEO - White Dragon Warrior Society
President - Glenn Wilson's Martial Arts Academies International
Head Coach - Wilson's "Pai Lum Tao" Warriors Team USA
Published author
Film Fight Choreographer

Professor:
Gong Yuen Chuan Fa Family

Masters Certifications in:
Chin Kon Pai Meditation
Pai Te Lung Chuan Kung Fu
Bok Leen Pai Kenpo
Pai Yung Tai Chi Chuan
Quan Nien Chi Kung
Shaolin Chuan Fa / Moi Fah Kung Fu

Proud member of:
Gong Yuen Chuan Fa Federation
White Dragon Warrior Society, Inc.
World Kuoshu Federation
United States Chinese Kuoshu Federation
Pai Lum White Dragon / White Lotus Society
World Head of Family Sokeship Council
Martial Arts Collective Society
Pan China Confederation Martial Arts – Beijing, China
International Chinese Kempo Karate Federation

Grandmaster Wilson is a senior disciple of the late Great Grandmaster Dr. Daniel Kane Pai and was chosen by Dr. Pai to head up The White Dragon Warrior Society and carry on the Pai Lum Tao torch of learning. Glenn now dedicates his martial arts life to keeping the dreams of Daniel Kane Pai alive and educating the world to this most fascinating style.

Grandmaster Wilson has had a truly illustrious career. As a competitor in the seventies he was a member of the U.S. Team and won five world titles and eight U.S. National titles. In the eighties he served for four years as a coach on the U.S. Team. Grandmaster Wilson has appeared in virtually every major Martial Arts magazine and has been voted into 6 Martial Arts Hall of Fames. His book "Pai Lum Tao - Way of the White Dragon" was published by Unique Publications and is the first book ever published on the Pai Lum Tao system.

As a personal protection specialist he has secured the safety of such celebrities as Michael Jackson, Dolly Parton, Charles Barkley, Larry Bird, Dianna Ross, The Beach Boys, The Righteous Brothers, Huey Lewis, Liza Minneli, Barbara Mandrel, Larry King, Don 'The Dragon' Wilson, General Swartzkoff and many more.

He has appeared in and served as fight choreographer for action movies such as Don (The Dragon's) movie - Redemption in the United States and the movie Shaolin Kid in Europe. At this time in his life he keeps busy as a corporate Director of Security / Investigations, Personal Protection Specialist, Crises Intervention Instructor, and President of Glenn Wilson's Martial Arts Academies International which are presently located in North America, Central America, Caribbean, Europe and Africa and is absolutely the largest Pai Lum Martial Arts organization in the world! He also serves as Grandmaster and CEO of the largest Pai Lum Tao organization in the world.

Grandmaster Wilson has been training in the martial arts for more than forty eight years. On Glenn's 10th birthday he began what would become a lifelong devotion to martial arts. He started in Kodokan Judo and studied diligently to perform the graceful yet brutal moves of this Japanese art.. When he was 16 he witnessed a Kenpo demonstration by Master Thomas Dunn that captivated him more than anything he'd ever experienced in the arts. The smooth, fluid and extremely powerful techniques mystified the young martial artist, who to this day holds a major reverence for its curriculum. Glenn studied the various Kenpo disciplines of Tracy's Kenpo, Shorinji Kempo, Kongo Do Kenpo, Chinese Kenpo and the style that would stay with him for life - Bok Leen Pai Kenpo.

He made the natural transition from his Kenpo roots to the various studies of Chuan Fa. Glenn trained in Gong Yuen Chuan Fa, Lo Han Chuan, Moi Fah Chuan, Five Animal methods, White Crane, and Pai Te Lung Chuan of Pai Lum Tao - a style that captured his imagination and gave new meaning to his martial arts pursuits. The internal influences that would help him center his life and training were practiced in Pai Lum Tao's systems of Pai Yung Tai Chi, Kuan Yin Chi Kung and Chin Kon Pai Meditation. Chin Kon Pai Meditation would become a practice that he has done faithfully daily for the past thirty plus years.

Glenn's life would change for the good in the mid seventies when he went from the private outdoor (very secluded) training of Master Jim Mcintosh to being accepted as a direct disciple of martial arts legend Great Grandmaster Dr. Daniel Kane Pai. Glenn was brought into the Pai Lum Tao System at the rank he held at the time in the Kou Shu of Taiwan - a third higher level black. This was a very rare happening and reserved for only the few warriors with honor, courage and an very high level of martial skill. Then in 1979 Dr. Pai elevated Glenn to Master and named him head of his family of Pai Lum Tao martial arts. That was ordained the 'Gong Yuen Chuan Fa' family of Pai Lum Tao Martial Arts.

Several years before Dr. Pai's passing he and his disciple, Glenn, formed the White Dragon Warrior Society. The formation was designed to preserve the traditions of Pai Lum Tao, share and strengthen the system and legitimize rank among the families. Dr. Pai served as the Chairman of the Board and Co-Founder, while Glenn was Vice Chairman of the Board of the White Dragon Warrior Society, Inc. (after Dr. Pai's passing Glenn became Chairman of the Board), President of Glenn Wilson's Martial Arts Academies International, and Head Coach of the Wilson's Warriors Competition/ Demonstration Team.

Great Grandmaster Pai died in 1993. This left Grandmaster Glenn C. Wilson in charge of the Society they formed - the White Dragon Warrior Society - as well as Senior Master of his "own" Family of Pai Lum Tao. Glenn travels the world teaching the different 'Pai' systems of Asian arts. Known as a great martial artist, he reveres the teachings and practice of Chin Kon Pai Meditation close to his heart.

Glenn Wilson is considered a grandmaster's grandmaster. He is what a Grandmaster should be: He doesn't talk the game; he lives the life - A Pai Lum Tao Way of Life. I am proud to call him my Pai Lum Brother for more than 35 years. He has been a teacher, brother, and a traditional guru in its highest level.
Master Level – Don 'The Dragon' Wilson

Dyan Chan Zen

Dhyan is, as it is known in India, the birthplace of the practice to contemplate. There was a seed that was waiting to grow and be nourished. Over many centuries Dhyan did not grow despite its treasure to mankind. To be nourished and eventually grow it had to leave its place of birth, so it did.

With time, travel, exposure and acceptance it eventually would grow in China. There it became known as Chan and grew quickly and widely throughout the lands. With a people that strived for balance the teachings of Chan was seen as a positive aid to peoples everyday life and struggles. Thousands of buildings would be erected for people to practice and for teachers to scribe their thoughts. Yet it could not blossom fully.

It needed a new exposure and people's philosophy to receive what it needed to mature and fully blossom. It was finally time for the beautiful plant to come to full blossom in the land of Japan and became known as Zen. The people of the islands were very receptive and welcoming to the new philosophies, this was the birth of Zen. In the hearts of the progressive people of Japan they were searching to move forward yet maintain the traditions of the ancestors.

Dhyan

ध्यान के रूप में यह भारत, विचार करने के लिए अभ्यास के जन्मस्थान में जाना जाता है. एक बीज है कि विकसित करने के लिए इंतज़ार कर रहा था और मनुष्य होना था. कई सदियों से यह मानव जाति के लिए अपने खजाने के बावजूद विकसित नहीं किया था. मनुष्य और अंततः बढ़ने के अपने जन्म स्थान छोड़ना पड़ा है, तो यह किया है.

Chan

随着时间的推移，旅游，接触和接受它最终将在中国发展。

在那里，它被称为陈增长迅速而广泛地通过了土地。

随着人们争取平衡的教诲，陈被看作是一个积极的帮助到人们

的日常生活和斗争。成千上万的建筑物将被竖立人的实践和

教师划线他们的想法。然而，它不能开花充分。

Chapter 1 - Introduction

Zen

これは、新しい暴露し、それが成熟しており、完全に開花するために必要なものを受け取るために人々の哲学を必要としていました。それは日本の地で満開に来て美しい植物のための最終的な時間だったと禅として知られるようになった。島の人々は非常に受容的であったし、新しい哲学を歓迎し、これは禅の誕生であった。日本の進歩的な人々の心の中で、彼らは祖先の伝統を維持する維持する前進して探していた。

Chapter 2

Philosophy

Chapter 2 - Philosophy

Philosophy

A proper attitude is crucial for proper progress. A person who thinks he knows everything usually knows nothing or just enough to get themselves hurt. To study Chin Kon Pai Meditation, an apprentice must practice patience, courage, perseverance and above all else humbleness.

A learner must start slowly, and not expect success in reaching their desired level of meditational state overnight. If a practitioner tries too hard, too fast, and does not accept the gradual change of mind, body & spirit, they will become frustrated and lose course in their journey.

Many new students want to be like a Master, but few have the perseverance and patients to reach such levels. If a student persists in a daily program, lightly at first, they can attain success in their own time and pace. There is no established time period that one must follow. It has been said by the masters that ones own journey is indeed the goal itself.

Surely it is worth the effort, for proficiency brings health, happiness, insight and confidence. And remember no practitioner can become an expert without first learning how to understand the way of things.

The abilities to become a skilled practitioner of meditation can take years or a lifetime. But the journey is truly worth the efforts. All of us must find the peace that is learned on our journey and apply it to our lives and hopefully spread our light to help others.

The practice of Chin Kon Pai Meditation is an awakening of ones mental, physical and spiritual existence. Its teachings focus on a higher level of ones achievement in life. The training of meditation has been proven through the experiences of practitioners for centuries. Many have found that the 'thinking exercise called meditation' truly becomes an avenue of awareness where one may achieve their goals in life. The 'Tao' of Chin Kon Pai Meditation is wisdom, enlightenment, principle, spiritual strength, purity and all comprehension.

Meditation is not a new craze or happening within our social structures worldwide. The greatest teachers of our world's history were avid practitioners of various forms of meditation. Jesus Christ, Buddha, David, Gandhi are a few of the most revered and loved leaders to find their guidance through meditation / prayer.

Practitioners of meditation are trained to know themselves and their surroundings. It is believed that this gives purpose to life and ones direction to follow. Once a person has started their journey, they begin to focus positive energy into their everyday thoughts and actions and their daily routines. This will open new doors of enlightenment and happiness. Is that not what we seek - happiness? That emotion must start within our own beings and that begins with thought. Meditation is truly the exercise of thought within our own minds to take us to levels of happiness and enlightenment that we desire.

Our philosophical look at mediation must be a simple one. We are who we are and choose to be. We are subjects to the laws of nature and the subjection of mankind. Our relationships with others must begin with the state of mind that we propagate. We control that state by thought and exercising the most powerful tool we possess, our minds. Yes, we are back to the very basics of our existence and being through meditation. With that, everyday we go forth to seek the Tao and the void, understanding ourselves and finding peace within ourselves. This peace we must share with others, and then they have the responsibility to do the same.

Challenge

When the bitter cold blows in from the North, the snow engulfs Mother Earth sending all into a state of hibernation, the lotus flower blooms, sharing its beauty to all. The endurance, beauty, durability, and strength of the white lotus have made it a symbol of reverence throughout Asia. Within the practice of Chin Kon Pai Meditation we visualize the purity, strength and power of our own minds. Our minds are not so different than the beautiful and powerful white lotus flower. When all around it is failing and decaying, it has the ability to grow and maintains its beauty and strength. With this meditational practice we know we can overcome all challenges we face. That alone is a great form of peace and resolve.

What is the nature of my challenge?

Is it different from my last challenge?

How do I approach my challenge?

How would someone else view my challenge?

How do I feel about this challenge?

What do I know about this challenge?

When do I start doing something to resolve this challenge?

Do I really need to solve this challenge?

Does there really exist a challenge?

Let me now visualize this challenge.

May I seek a wise solution to this disillusion called a challenge?

Solutions to challenges are found in the practice of Honor, Loyalty, Courage coupled within the Mind, Body and Spirit. This is the ancient cycle and continuation of enlightenment and self peace.

A Good Student

A good walker leaves no tracks

A good speaker makes no slips

A good listener forgets nothing

A good strike never misses its mark

A good body never tires of technique

A good technique never requires explanation

A good student seeks none

The Ancient Masters

The Ancient Masters were subtle, mysterious,

silent, profound and responsive

Watchful, like men crossing a winter stream

Alert, like men in the jungle

Courteous, like visiting guests

Yielding, like melting ice

Simple, like uncarved wood

Hollow, like caves

The Ancient Masters were aware that the flesh

dies away and is soon forgotten

The spirit remains forever

The Tao

The Tao cannot be defined by words
Any words used are one-sided and therefore misleading
Tao is merely a word given to the nameless source of the Universe
The Universe is the mother of all things, visible and invisible
When you have ceased judging things by yourself
You may see the unseen
Judging things by their relationship to you, you see the visible
But visible and invisible are only words that are different by definition
In essence they are the same
This mystery is a shadow within absolute darkness
Here is the doorway to truth
All things are one
The Tao smooths the rough surface of life, like gentle rain
The perfect way 'Tao' is without difficulty,
Save that which avoids picking and choosing
If you quest for the plain truth
Be not concerned with right or wrong
The conflict is a sickness of the mind

Thoughts

The heart of a fool is in his mouth, but the mouth of the wise man is in his heart.

After all this is over, all that will really have mattered is how we treated each other.

They may forget what you said, but they will never forget how you made them feel.

Better bend than break.

There is never time to do it right, but there is always time to do it over.

Facts do not cease to exist because they are ignored.

Fail to plan, plan to fail.

Be of sound mind, good judgment and superior moral character then you may adhere to your own free will.

As a practitioner of meditation I shall progress, therefore I will never condemn, ridicule, embarrass or shame others.

I shall never do anything that would be inconsistent with my moral, social or religious beliefs.

Through meditation I will find my minds message for life.

Chapter 2 - Philosophy
Care of Oneself

For years I have sought enlightenment, said the disciple. I feel I am near it and want to know how to take the next step.

A man who knows how to seek enlightenment knows also how to take care of himself. How do you support yourself asked the master?

That is just a detail. I have rich parents who help me along my spiritual path. Because of that, I can dedicate myself entirely to sacred things.

Very well – said the master. I will explain to you the next step: look at the sun for half a minute.

The disciple obeyed.

When he had finished, the master asked him describe the landscape around him.

I can't. The sun's brightness dazzled my eyes.

A man who looks fixedly at the sun ends up blind. A man who only looks for Light, and shifts his responsibilities onto the shoulders of others, never finds what he is seeking was the master's comment.

Dragon's Code

I am what I am because I choose to Be. I am a Dragon by choice, and Subject to it's laws. My brothers and sisters are my heart and my mind. Even though we may disagree with each other, we still strive to be one. Forgetting all categories and letting energy that wishes to exist, exist. But as a Dragon, I must go forth To seek the Tao and the void, Understanding myself, and finding Peace within.

By Great Grand Master Daniel Kane Pai

English

Das Dragon Gesetz

Ich bin was Ich bin, weil Ich es so wollte. Ich bin ein Dragon bei Wunsch und ein Subject seinem Gesetz. Meine Brüder und Schwestern sind mein Herz und meine Gedanken. Auch wenn wir nicht immer einer Meinung sind, bemühen wir uns doch einig zu sein. Wir vergessen alle Categorieren und lassen die erwünschten Energien existieren. Als ein Dragon muß ich vorwärts gehen um den Tao zu suchen, mich selbst zu verstehen, und Frieden in mir selbst zu finden.

German

Dragon's Code

Tá mé cad tá mé mar gheall ar a roghnaigh mé a bheith. Tá mé Dragon de rogha, agus Faoi réir sé dlíthe. Tá mo chuid dearthái-reacha agus deirfiúra-cha mo chroí agus mo intinn. Cé is féidir linn a n-aontaíonn le chéile, déanaimid ár ndícheall i gcónaí a bheith ar cheann. Forgetting gach catagóir agus ligean fuinnimh gur mian a bheith ann, ann. Ach mar Dragon, ní mór dom dul amach a lorg TAO agus ar neamhní, a thuiscint féin, agus aimsiú Síochána laistigh de.

Gaelic

Codigo de los Dragones

Yo soy lo que soy, porque yo lo elegi, yo soy un dragon por la opción y conforme a sus leyes. Mis hermanos y hermanas son mi corazón y mi mente. Aun puede haber discrepancia entre uno y otro, todavía nos esforzamos en ser uno. Olvidándose de todas las categorias y dejando la energía que desea existir, que exista. Pero como un dragón yo debo ir hacia adelante y buscar el tao y el vacío, entendiendome a mi mismo y encontrando paz interna.

Spanish

Código do Dragão

Eu sou o que eu sou, porque eu escolho ser. Eu sou um dragão por opção, e sujeito a ela as leis. Meus irmãos e irmãs são meu coração e minha mente. Embora possamos discordar uns com os outros, ainda se esforçar para ser um. Esquecendo todas as categorias e deixando que a energia que deseja existir, existe. Mas, como um dragão, devo sair para buscar o Tao e do vazio, compreender-me, e encontrar a paz interior.

Portuguese

The Dragon Code

Jag är vad jag är för att jag väljer att vara. Jag är en drake genom val, och under förutsättning att det är lagar. Mina bröder och systrar är mitt hjärta och mitt sinne. Även om vi kanske inte håller med varandra, strävar vi fortfarande vara en. Att glömma alla kategorier och låta energi som önskar finns existera. Men som en drake, måste jag gå ut för att söka Tao och tomrummet, förstå mig själv, och hitta fred inom.

Swedish

The Dragon's Code

Ik ben wat ik ben want ik kies om te Zijn. Ik ben een draak naar keuze en met inachtneming van het is wetten. Mijn broers en zussen zijn mijn hart en mijn verstand. Hoewel we misschien niet eens met elkaar, we nog steeds naar streven een te zijn. Vergeten alle categorieën en laten energie die wil bestaan bestaan,. Maar als een draak, ik moet uitgaan naar de Tao en de leegte te zoeken, begrijpen zelf, en het vinden van vrede in.

Dutch

Chapter 2 - Philosophy
The Dragon's Code

白龍道
龍的格言

做龍，就要遵守這準則，我的弟兄姊妹我就是我，因定是我的選擇，我選擇就是我的心和智。雖然我們間中不妥協，但我們仍然團結一致。忘記你有分歧，而由原動力去生存，去發揚光大。但由於我是龍，我務必要去尋找那道與道之間的真紳，明白自我又尋找內裡太平。

Chinese

I Am

I am because of the nights and days I have seen
I believe I am a man for the things I have
done: But all it is, is just feelings of
sensations that are created by my
mind: Those that I touch
know me as I am, these
simple arts that are called
Kung Fu are feelings I
have of the things I now
love: These high sensations
and thrills of my spine,
are not love but a
practitioner's body, that
cares for his art, if I
sound as if I am a
dreamer... Then let me
dream as I practice this
martial art that is called
Kung Fu, These strange
Feelings I have of knowing
The world, Devotion.

By Great Grandmaster Dr. Daniel Kane Pai

Chapter 2 - Philosophy

Miao Xing's Teachings

One must not use his power for deception of people,

One must not rise over other people,

One must not use this art for suppression of people,

If there are achievements there should be flaws,

It is necessary to know about flaws to attain higher achievements

It is necessary to breed the true greatness of spirit

White Dragon's Flame

Look into the flame of the candle

Concentrate, search for its center

Now calm your spirit, what do you see

Peace or discontent, I see both Grandmaster

What you see my son is your own heart

Train yourself harder like an incessant storm

You tell your American students to seek peace always

But you must first find peace yourself

If you do as I say, you will have true power

And the flame will reflect only content

Life and Death

A man is born gentle and weak

At his death he is stiff and hard

Green plants are tender and filled with sap

At their death they are withered and dry

Therefore the stiff and unbending is the disciple of death

The gentle and yielding, the disciple of life

Thus an army without flexibility never wins a battle

A tree that does not bend with wind will break

Power

In a pursuit of true power

a student must reach deep within the mind

No longer with human weakness

You identify with the power of the Tiger

Through the flow of Chi life force

To accomplish this, you must meditate

Strengthen the muscles and bones and read the Tao

To be at one with all nature

You must be at one with yourself

True power is a combining of psychic and physical principles

that are attained through hard training

Words of Wisdom For All

Words of Jesus

"So don't worry about tomorrow, for tomorrow will bring its own worries. Today's trouble is enough for today."

"Do to others whatever you would like them to do to you."

"And so I tell you, keep on asking, and you will receive what you ask for. Keep on seeking, and you will find. Keep on knocking, and the door will be opened to you. For everyone who asks, receives. Everyone who seeks, finds. And to everyone who knocks, the door will be opened."

"What shall it profit a man if he gains the whole world but loses his soul."

"For we walk by faith, not by sight."

"The good man brings good things out of the good stored up in his heart, and the evil man brings evil things out of the evil stored up in his heart. For out of the overflow of his heart his mouth speaks."

"No one lights a lamp and puts it in a place where it will be hidden, or under a bowl. Instead he puts it on its stand, so that those who come in may see the light."

"If you bring forth what is within you, what you bring forth will save you. If you do not bring forth what is within you, what you do not bring forth will destroy you."

Words of the Dalai Lama

"Our own brain, our own heart is our temple."

"Open your arms to change, but don't let go of your values."

"Happiness is not something ready made. It comes from your own actions."

"We can never obtain peace in the outer world until we make peace with ourselves."

"Be kind whenever possible, it is always possible."

"I find hope in the darkest of days, and focus in the brightest. I do not judge the universe."

"Where ignorance is our master, there is no possibility of real peace."

"If you don't love yourself, you cannot love others. You will not be able to love others. If you have no compassion for yourself then you are not able of developing compassion for others."

"With realization of one's own potential and self-confidence in one's ability, one can build a better world."

"Love and compassion are necessities, not luxuries. Without them humanity cannot survive."

"Sometimes one creates a dynamic impression by saying something, and sometimes one creates as significant an impression by remaining silent."

"It is very important to generate a good attitude, a good heart, as much as possible. From this, happiness in both the short term and the long term for both yourself and others will come."

Words of Confucius

Before you embark on a journey of revenge, dig two graves.

Everything has its beauty but not everyone sees it.

Forget injuries, never forget kindnesses.

I hear and I forget. I see and I remember. I do and I understand.

It does not matter how slowly you go so long as you do not stop.

Respect yourself and others will respect you.

Study the past if you would define the future.

When we see men of a contrary character, we should turn inwards and examine ourselves.

Wheresoever you go, go with all your heart.

By nature, men are nearly alike; by practice, they get to be wide apart.

Hold faithfulness and sincerity as first principles.

Words of Lao Tzu

"Watch your thoughts; they become words. Watch your words; they become actions. Watch your actions; they become habit. Watch your habits; they become character. Watch your character; it becomes your destiny."

"Simplicity, patience, compassion. These three are your greatest treasures. Simple in actions and thoughts, you return to the source of being. Patient with both friends and enemies, you accord with the way things are. Compassionate toward yourself, you reconcile all beings in the world."

"Knowing others is intelligence; knowing yourself is true wisdom. Mastering others is strength; mastering yourself is true power. If you realize that you have enough, you are truly rich."

"Those who know do not speak. Those who speak do not know."

"Life is a series of natural and spontaneous changes. Don't resist them; that only creates sorrow. Let reality be reality. Let things flow naturally forward in whatever way they like."

"When I let go of what I am, I become what I might be."

"The truth is not always beautiful, nor beautiful words the truth."

"Time is a created thing. To say 'I don't have time,' is like saying, 'I don't want to."

"Nature does not hurry, yet everything is accomplished."

"Be content with what you have; rejoice in the way things are."

"When you realize there is nothing lacking, the whole world belongs to you."

"Be careful what you water your dreams with. Water them with worry and fear and you will produce weeds that choke the life from your dream. Water them with optimism and solutions and you will cultivate success. Always be on the lookout for ways to turn a problem into an opportunity for success. Always be on the lookout for ways to nurture your dream."

"A man with outward courage dares to die; a man with inner courage dares to live."

"Because one believes in oneself, one doesn't try to convince others. Because one is content with oneself, one doesn't need others' approval. Because one accepts oneself, the whole world accepts him or her."

"The best fighter is never angry."

"At the center of your being you have the answer;

you know who you are and you know what you want."

"If you do not change direction, you may end up where you are heading."

"If you understand others you are smart.

If you understand yourself you are illuminated.

If you overcome others you are powerful.

If you overcome yourself you have strength.

If you know how to be satisfied you are rich.

If you can act with vigor, you have a will.

If you don't lose your objectives you can be long-lasting.

If you die without loss, you are eternal."

Words of Mozi

"A person will naturally follow the right way when under good influence."

"Would a lover of beauty say 'No one in my family loves it, so I will not either?'"

"Universal love leads to mutual benefit, just as a son would love and honor others' parents so that the latter's sons would honor and love his parents."

"Ordinary people are tinged in the same way as sages."

Words of Siddhartha Gautama 'Buddha'

"Thousands of candles can be lit from a single candle, and the life of the candle will not be shortened. Happiness never decreases by being shared."

"All that we are is the result of what we have thought. The mind is everything. What we think we become."

"You will not be punished for your anger, you will be punished by your anger."

We are shaped by our thoughts; we become what we think. When the mind is pure, joy follows like a shadow that never leaves."

"Three things cannot be long hidden: the sun, the moon, and the truth."

"You yourself, as much as anybody in the entire universe, deserve your love and affection."

"The mind is everything. What you think you become."

"The only real failure in life is not to be true to the best one knows."

"A jug fills drop by drop."

"However many holy words you read, However many you speak, What good will they do you If you do not act on upon them?"

"An idea that is developed and put into action is more important than an idea that exists only as an idea."

"The tongue like a sharp knife, kills without drawing blood."

"Even death is not to be feared by one who has lived wisely."

"Work out your own salvation. Do not depend on others."

"Your work is to discover your work and then with all your heart to give yourself to it."

"The secret of health for both mind and body is not to mourn for the past, worry about the future, or anticipate troubles, but to live in the present moment wisely and earnestly."

"No one saves us but ourselves. No one can and no one may. We ourselves must walk the path."

"A generous heart, kind speech, and a life of service and compassion are the things which renew humanity."

"The way is not in the sky. The way is in the heart."

"Every human being is the author of his own health or disease."

"Hatred does not cease through hatred at any time. Hatred ceases through love. This is an unalterable law."

"There has to be evil so that good can prove its purity above it."

"To keep the body in good health is a duty...otherwise we shall not be able to keep our mind strong and clear."

"Better than a thousand hollow words, is one word that brings peace."

"To conquer oneself is a greater task than conquering others"

"What we think, we become."

Osho Thoughts About Laughter

Laughter is not irreligious. Laughter is one of the most evolved phenomena in human life. No other animal can laugh, it is only man; it is only man who can laugh.

In a real deep laughter the mind disappears. It is not a part of mind or of the heart. When a real laughter happens -- a belly laughter, as it is called -- then it comes from your very core; from your very center ripples start spreading towards your circumference. Just as you throw a rock into a silent lake and ripples arise and they start moving towards the source, in the same way real laughter arises from your center and moves towards your circumference. It is almost like an earthquake! Each single cell of your body, each fiber dances in tune.

Laughter has never been used as a meditation. I may be the first person who is using laughter as a meditation. Jokes have never been used as part of a spiritual transformation -- I may be the first person! But they can be used; they are tremendously refreshing.

Laughter is a great medicine. It is a tremendously powerful therapy. If you can laugh at your own unconscious, the unconscious loses its force. In your very laughter your guilt, your wounds will disappear.

My own experience says to me that if you can laugh rightly, in the right moment, it will bring you out of unconsciousness into the open sky, from the darkness to the light. I am introducing laughter as a meditation because nothing makes you so total as laughter; nothing makes you stop your thinking as laughter does. Just for a moment you are no more a mind. Just for a moment you are no more in time. Just for a moment you have entered into another space where you are total and whole and healed.

Laughter is beautiful when it comes out of understanding, out of innocence. But when it is hysterical it is insane and stupid.

If you really want to laugh you will have to learn how to weep. If you cannot weep and if you are not capable of tears, you will become incapable of laughter. A man of laughter is also a man of tears -- then a man is balanced. A man of bliss is also a man of silence. A man who is ecstatic is also a man who is centered. They both go together. And out of this togetherness of polarities a balanced being is born. And that is what the goal is.

When you become a calm and cool observer of life you are going to laugh -- not ordinary laughter but a belly laughter like a lion's roar. And white lotuses will start showering on you. Life is neither serious nor nonserious. It is a tremendous play, playfulness.

Laughter brings some energy from your inner source to your surface. Energy starts flowing, follows laughter like a shadow. Have you watched it? When you really laugh, for those few moments you are in a deep meditative state. Thinking stops. It is impossible to laugh and think together. They are diametrically opposite: either you can laugh or you can think. If you really laugh, thinking stops. If you are still thinking, laughter will be just so-so, it will be just so-so, lagging behind. It will be a crippled laughter.

When you really laugh, suddenly mind disappears. And the whole Zen methodology is how to get into no-mind -- laughter is one of the beautiful doors to get to it.

If you are possessed by laughter, thinking stops. And if you know a few moments of no-mind, those glimpses will promise you many more rewards that are going to come. You just have to become more and more of the sort, of the quality. More and more, thinking has to be dropped. Laughter can be a beautiful introduction to a non-thinking state. And the beauty is.... There are methods -- for example, you can concentrate on a flame or on a black dot, or you can concentrate on a mantra, but the greater possibility is that by the time the mind is disappearing you will start feeling sleepy, you will fall asleep. Because before the mind disappears there open two alternatives: sleep and satori.

In some Zen monasteries, every monk has to start his morning with laughter, and has to end his night with laughter -- the first thing and the last thing!

Laughter is one of the things most repressed by society all over the world, in all the ages. Society wants you to be serious. Parents want their children to be serious, teachers want their students to be serious, the bosses want their servants to be serious, the commanders want their armies to be serious. Seriousness is required of everybody. They may feel that laughter is dangerous and rebellious, it is not.

Do Not Stand At My Grave And Weep.

Do not stand at my grave and weep.

I am not there, I do not sleep.

I am a thousand winds that blow.

I am the diamond glints on the snow.

I am the sunlight on the ripened grain.

I am the gentle Autumn's rain.

When you awaken in the morning hush,

I am the swift uplifting rush,

of quiet birds in circled flight.

I am the soft star that shines at night.

Do not stand at my grave and cry.

I am not there, I did not die.

My soul is still alive in you.

Your best is what I expect from you.

Good things never really die,

They go on and on, like you and I.

By: Dr. Daniel Kalimaahaae Kane Pai

Chapter 3

What Is Meditation?

Chapter 3 - What is Meditation 53

What is Meditation?

In Europe and the Western Hemisphere, the word "meditation" comes from Latin and means "thinking." "To meditate" is "to think." Thinking is a natural, normal process in which most individuals engage every waking moment as well as throughout much of their sleep. Most people would be surprised to find that they already practice some degree of meditation!

The difference between the practitioners of any particular type of meditation and non-practitioners is that, during at least some part of the day or week, the meditator takes time out to think about one particular thing. The practitioner chooses the object of their thoughts, focusing on a particular thought, subject, emotion, activity, or experience. Even the meditator's own consciousness may become the focus of their practice.

The amount of time meditating or the frequency of meditation is not what makes the practitioner. Practitioners of meditation differ in regards to their interests and conditions. These differences are reflected in their choice of schools of meditation and philosophy. The determining factor is simply that the practitioner has made the effort to focus, concentrate, and direct his or her thoughts and thinking.

The thoughts of the non-practitioner may jump from one thought to the next. The non-practitioner may believe that they are doing the thinking, but their thoughts are reactions, products of both internal and external conditions.

When the mind and/or body are restless or agitated, what feels like a poor or light meditation will help the mind and body to rest, and is especially strengthening in what might be future difficult times. Do not compare meditation sessions by how you feel afterwards. It takes more effort to meditate during bad times even thought the experience of the "meditative state" may seem to be absent. In all forms of meditation the mind drifts off. When we catch ourselves being distracted, we return our awareness to whatever was the focal point of meditation. We are practicing the return to point or center of meditation. Weathering the bad days, with each return we are strengthening the mental concentration. Many times the bad days give us a better practice, even though we may not feel satisfied with our session.

The commonalities of the various types of meditation are much greater than are their differences. Many times as humans we tend to dwell on differences, even though one purpose of meditation is to transcend differences.

Several systems for "classifying" types of meditation are used. While these systems may seem to help in the beginning, they eventually become a boundary that the one must overcome. Three methods of classification are: structure, way and path.

Methods of meditation may be either structured or unstructured. In a structured meditation, the activities performed are carefully and precisely defined.

The practitioner is instructed in regards to the correct focus of meditation, the nature of any incorrect focuses of meditation, and the processes used in the meditation.

Forms of meditation that have continued some connection with their founding traditions require that the practitioner prepare themselves in some specific manner before meditating. Many times, preparation includes some form of mental-spiritual and/or physical cleansing in order to purify the body, mind, and soul. Proper preparation may have several purposes. It may be believed that the practitioner needs to be purified, cleansed or made worthy. It may be viewed that preparation shows that the practitioner is making personal efforts in order to be worthy of the meditation experience. Preparation may be seen as helping to clear away false or preconceived notions so that the practitioner does not "contaminate" their experience.

Psychological preparation may help the practitioner start a process of focusing more on the meditation and less on any worldly or distracting concerns. This may be especially true if the practitioner meditates with some frequency and always performs the same rites or activities beforehand. These activities serve as stimuli to slow down the body and mind so that one may enter a meditative state. To some extent, the preparation may become the beginning of the meditation itself.

Before a meditation session, address the following questions:

• Have you selected practice times during which you are relatively unlikely to be distracted?

• Have you finished some other duty that would distract you if it were not finished?

• Do you have a special quiet place in which to practice?

• Try to make sure that you won't be interrupted.

• Do not have a drink containing caffeine (coffee, tea, cola, and some non-cola soft drinks) for at least 2 hours before practicing. Caffeine can make it more difficult to relax and focus your attention on what you are doing.

• You should not eat any food for at least an hour before practicing.

• When you are finished, come out of your relaxed state very slowly and gently. Take about 60 seconds to easily open your eyes all the way. Then stretch and take a deep breath.

Now go forth with your meditation and conquer your challenges with the power of love & light.

Dhyan Chan Zen Tao

What is Dhyan Chan Zen Tao in today's world? In the Pai Lum Tao Asian arts this simply means in English to contemplate and reflect on our thoughts and feelings. Even at best this is a rough translation for it may not be the same for you and certainly is not the same for all. What really matters is the outcome of the process or exercise practiced.

Dhyan is as it is known in India, the birthplace of the practice to contemplate. There was a seed that was waiting to grow and be nourished. With time, travel, exposure and acceptance it eventually would grow in China.

In China it became known as Chan and grew quickly and widely throughout the lands. With a people that strived for balance the teachings of Chan was seen as a positive aid to peoples everyday life and struggles. Thousands of buildings would be erected for people to practice and for teachers to scribe their thoughts.

Then it would be time for the beautiful plant to come to full blossom in the land of Japan. The people of the islands of Ryu Kyu were very receptive and welcoming to the Chan philosophies, this was the birth of Zen. In the hearts of the progressive people of the islands they were searching to move forward yet maintain the traditions of the ancestors.

The Tao 'philosophical way' of meditation in Pai Lum Tao Martial Arts is Zen. This makes up approximately sixty percent of the Chin Kon Pai practice. The other thoughts of practice are twenty percent Chakra meditation training and twenty percent Guided meditation exercise. Through the teachings of the ancestors of Pai Lum Tao to the modern emerging of Dr. Daniel Kalimaahaae Kane Pai's wisdom the tranquility inside is passed on to generations of students.

Chapter 3 - What is Meditation

Chapter 4

Elements of Chin Kon Pai Meditation

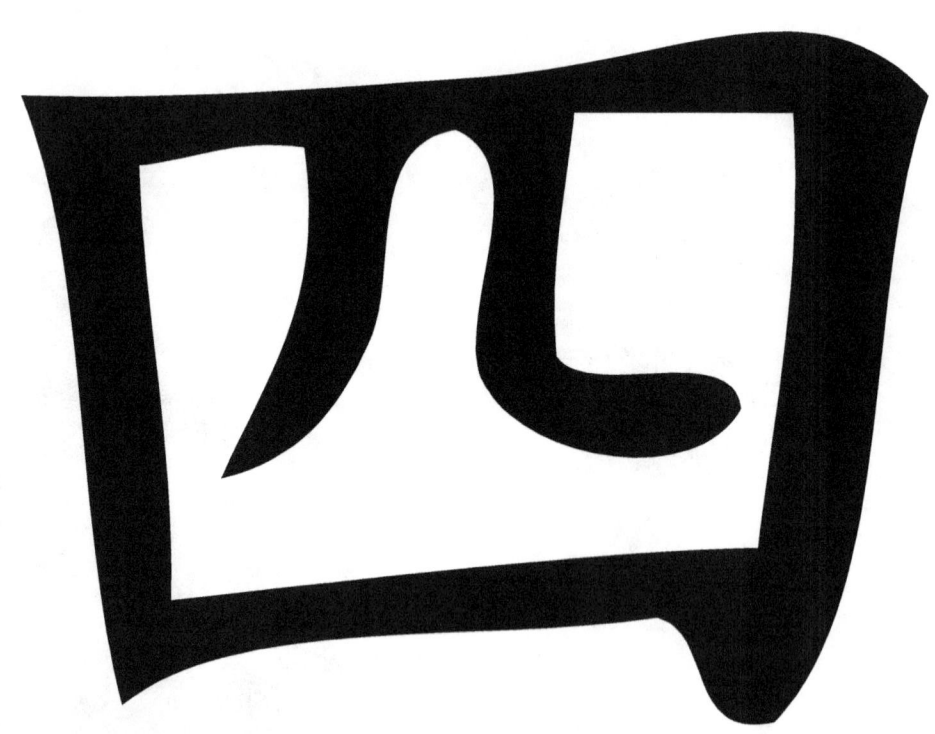

Chapter 4 - Elements of Chin Kon Pai Meditation

Elements Of Meditation

Meditation is often utilized as an exercise for connecting with your inner self or your higher power, in an attempt to liberate your mind and body from stress, anxieties or fears. Meditation is the capability to rid oneself of negative energy within your mind, body and spirit. For many people the goal of meditation is to convert negative energy into positive / productive energy. Many times this can be used to act as healing benefits for disease, illness, stress, anxiety, and fears of all natures. When practiced regularly meditation offers clarity and a sense of peace of mind. The benefits of meditation can result in therapeutic results for our three main areas of health - mental, physical and spiritual.

Mental challenges and disorders that may benefit through the regular practice of meditation are immense. Some of them are.

Stress

Depression

Panic attacks

Anxiety

Irritability and moodiness

Memory loss

Self esteem and self confidence

Social interaction and relationships

For enhanced physical wellbeing, meditation may assist in relief for the following.

Pain

Cancer

Heart disease

Angina pains

Asthma

PMS

Chronic Fatigue Syndrome

High blood pressure

Cholesterol

Scientists and doctors agree that the practice of meditation may have a direct impact with the way we perceive our brain to be 'wired'. In recent years, there has been a rise of the research of meditation and its effects on the brain and the heart.

Depression from an overload of stress may result in physical injuries as well as health disorders such as cardiovascular complications and heart disease. One can, through the regular practice of meditation, reduce several risks to such conditions by reducing the stress. It has been discovered that when your brain is tranquil, a vivid enhancement to your mental health occurs; this reduces the risks of poor physical wellbeing as well.

Many times we find that the Spiritual desires of people may become deeper and have a stronger impact by escalating the following:

Greater love and respect for all living existence.

Understanding of the endless existence of a higher power.

Feelings of a sense of Oneness with yourself.

Strong sense of worship.
Feeling of peace with self and others.

Wide-ranging feelings of well being.

A deeper feeling and comprehension of their own purpose.

Feeling of a deep, inner sense.

When we think of meditation we think of the traditional roots being found or originating in eastern cultures, primarily India, Japan, China and Tibet. Buddhism, Zen and Hinduism play a great role in meditation throughout the world as we know it in modern times. However meditation can be found in all religions. The Christian form of meditation can be defined as prayer. During prayer a Christian will think upon thoughts that are pleasing and/or needed to help out their lives or the state of others. So in essence prayer itself is a form of meditation as a Christian will speak to Christ, God or to Saints. A great misconception by some is that Christians can not or should not meditate, by the mere definition of meditation that makes little sense. During Chin Kon Pai meditation a Christian would contemplate the positive thoughts relating to their gifts from God. This would help alleviate or minimize their stress and negativity. Surely this must be seen as something good to all people no matter what their religious beliefs may be.

Most of us lead a normal life, thus things can become very hectic on a daily basis. Contemplating on ones career/work, family life, friends, and social life, it is easy for stress levels to become extremely high. This is something most of us deal with and for a short period of time we may be able to handle this stress level. We know from extended studies in Psychology and human behavior that stress is a natural mechanism to events in our lives.

We know that we must take care of something to ultimately rid ourselves of our unwanted stress. So that stress does not take control of us or even get the best of us we have learned to control it or rid ourselves of it, meditation is absolutely one of the best tools for this and is practiced by millions of people worldwide. Chin Kon Pai meditation is not difficult, you simply decide to do it and prepare yourself, space and props.

A: Wear Comfortable Clothing

An individual needs to be sure that they are wearing clothing that is comfortable and free of tight restrictions. Many practitioners choose to practice in the nude, this is absolutely the most 'non restricting' way, but it must be free of distractions. Most people wear something that feels good and does not restrict any movement and that they enjoy being in for an unlimited amount of time. Comfortable / light clothing does set the mood for relaxation and you may want to have your 'meditation clothing' near by for quick access.

B: Creating a Peaceful Environment

All practitioners should create and have their own special meditation place. You should find a location away from loud distractions and anything that become a stressor. You want to be sure you will not be interrupted by anyone or anything. Leave behind all of your modern electronic devices such as cell phones, televisions or alarms. You will want to create and maintain a very calm atmosphere, this is your special place and time. Turn down the lights or even turn them off and light candles if need be. Then, if you wish to, you may create whatever soothing sounds that will assist you in reaching your stage of relaxation.

C: Prepare & Set Up Your Props

It is time to set up your special place with the needed props. What type of meditation you choose will determine your choice of props. You may choose no props at all, that is fine and in line with the teachings of Chin Kon Pai as well. Often practitioners will choose to bring a meditation stool, chair, pillows, meditation mat or blankets. Comfort is very important and must set in motion your experience and be maintained during your meditation time. Scented candles and incense are often utilized to assist with ones senses and mood setting. Keep in mind that whatever your choice it must be what works for you.

Standing Meditation Stances

Standing Posture - Earth

Standing Posture - Fire

Chapter 4 - Elements of Chin Kon Pai Meditation

Standing Posture - Holding Earth

Standing Posture - Metal

Chapter 4 - Elements of Chin Kon Pai Meditation

Standing Posture - Prayer Hand

Standing Posture - Recycling

Standing Posture - Water

Standing Posture - White Lotus

Standing Posture - Wood

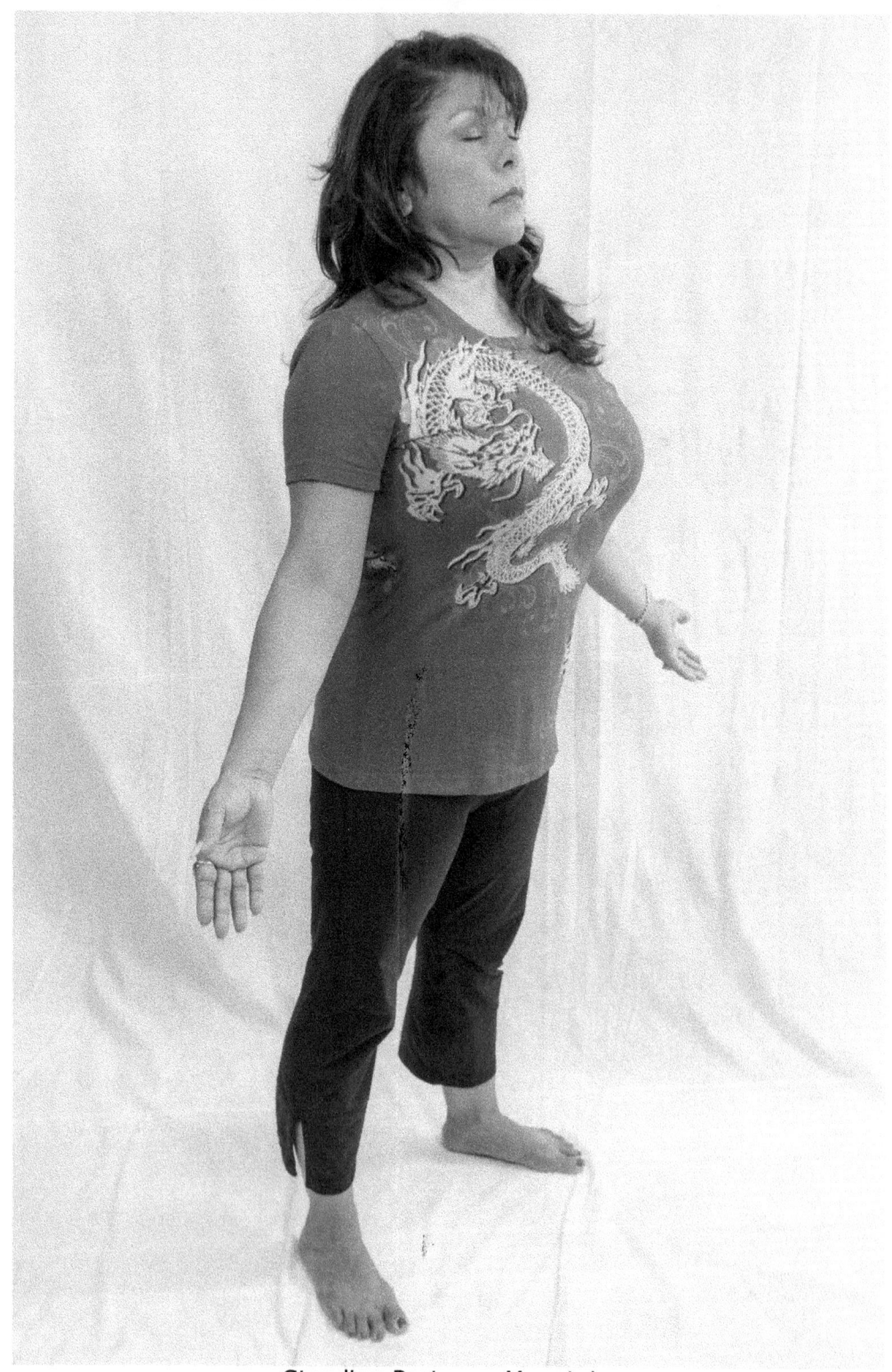

Standing Posture - Mountain

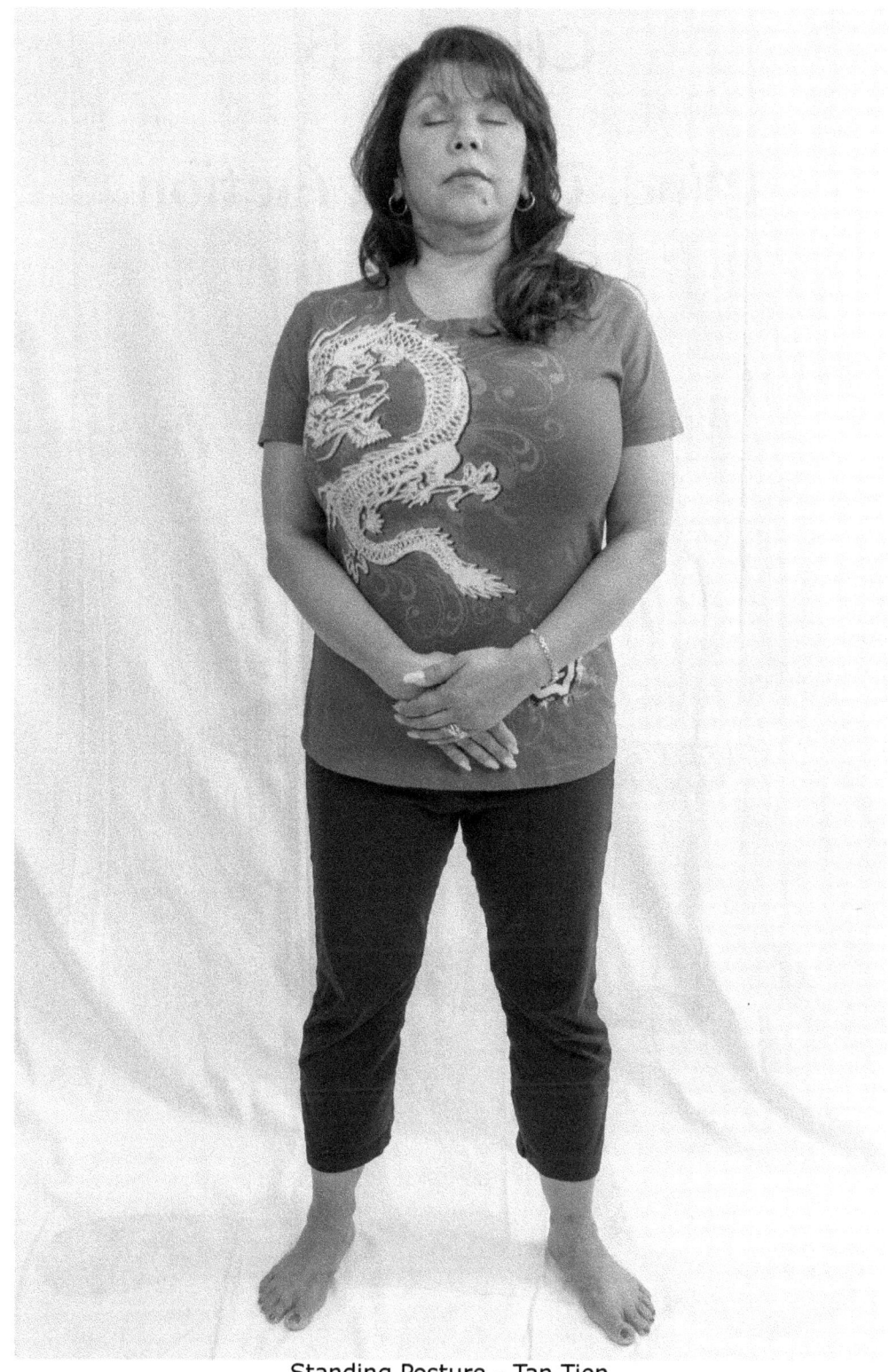

Standing Posture - Tan Tien

Chapter 5

Mind, Thought, Action

Chin Kon Pai Meditation is an accumulation of Dr. Daniel Kalimaahaae Kane Pai's many years of meditational study. These studies included a varied list of disciplines such as Chinese Buddhist, Japanese Zen, India's Vedic and Vipassana teachings, Hawaiian and Native American principles. The principles are simple and easy to follow and with a few minutes a day anyone can enhance their life. As a basic practice one will become a better person. If the practitioner wishes to continue to study the several levels of Chin Kon Pai Meditation they will quickly see that the studies will become more complex and challenging and with these elevated challenges will come heightened rewards in their development.

Practicing Chin Kon Pai Meditation techniques allows your mind to settle inward beyond external thought where one will experience the center of thought. This is our most peaceful level of consciousness — our innermost Self. Your body will experience a state of deep rest while your mind becomes increasingly alert. At this level your brain begins to function in a highly orderly and coherent manner. This is level one: the introduction to yourself and to the peace that you possess and that exists all around you.

You now may move to the next stage of consciousness, level two. Chin Kon Pai's level two teaches self-transformation through self-observation. It focuses on the deep interconnection between mind and body, which can be experienced through a focused attention to the physical sensations that form the life of the body, and that continuously interconnect and condition our mind. It is this observation-based, self-exploratory journey to the root of our mind and body that dissolves mental impurity. Once our impurities are diminished we can start to enjoy a more balanced mind full of love and compassion. The scientific laws that operate our thoughts, emotions, judgements and sensations become clearer. Through direct practice, the nature of how one grows or regresses, how one produces suffering or frees oneself from suffering is understood and life becomes clearer through increased awareness, self-control and a greater peace within.

Most people seek peace and harmony simply because these may be the very things we lack in our lives. From time to time all of us experience irritation, agitation, disharmony or suffering and when one suffers from agitation, one does not keep this misery limited to themselves. This negative energy will quickly be spread to others as well. The agitation creates the atmosphere around the miserable person. Most people who come into contact with them will feel the irritation and agitation as well.

If one lives at peace with themselves, they can live in peace with others around them. It starts with the individual because they have the choice. After all, human beings are social by nature, and we should not go against our nature. We live in societies and we are meant to live and deal with others. We must remain harmonious with ourselves and maintain peace and harmony around us, so that others can also live peacefully and harmoniously with us.

If one is negative or agitated it is because they have chosen to be negative or agitated. One must realize the basic reason or cause of the energy and choose to do something to overcome it. If one investigates the problem, it will become clear that whenever one starts generating any negativity in the mind, one is bound to become agitated. A negativity in the mind - a mental impurity - cannot exist with peace and harmony. It is a cancer of a sort, eating away at our power and strength. It will weaken us and if we allow this cancer to continue to manifest it will feed on our energy until it overcomes us.

Wise enlightened persons throughout history and around the world have studied the problems of negativity, human suffering, anger and hate, and they found a solution. If something unwanted happens and one reacts by generating anger, fear, or negativity they will only feed the very bad energy they wish to avoid. As soon as possible one should divert one's attention to something else, and then let their own good energy begin to overtake the bad. One way is to start repeating a word or a phrase, or some mantra - perhaps the name of a saintly person to whom you have devotion. The mind will be diverted and you will begin to think of a positive image that represents purity, strength and healing. Positive will overtake negative and you will feel the results immediately thereafter.

With this the mind feels free from anger and agitation. One should be aware that this solution works only at the conscious level. The anger, negativity and agitation have been driven deep into the unconscious area of the mind. At this level one continues to generate and multiply the same emotions. At the surface level there is a layer of peace and harmony, but in the depths of the mind there is a sleeping volcano of suppressed negativity which sooner or later will explode in a violent eruption.

This does not mean to run away from your challenges. The practice of Chin Kon Pai teaches us to control that which is around us with our thoughts and energy. Experience the reality of mind and matter within yourself, recognize that the problem is still there and that you are merely controlling it with your positive energy and power. This is the basis of controlling thought through intense meditational exercises. Escape is no solution: one must face the problem. Whenever negativity arises in the mind observe it, face it, and control it. As soon as one starts observing any mental defilement, they must begin to control it by casting it out, destroying it or temporarily sending it elsewhere. Keeping the negativity in the unconscious will not eradicate it; and allowing it to manifest in physical or vocal action will only magnify the problems. If one observes and lets a natural action take course, however, the negativity passes away and one has eradicated the bad energy.

The direct experience of one's own reality, our self-observation, is at the very root of Chin Kon Pai Meditation. One will practice what has become known as 'seeing with open eyes'; the practitioner is observing things as they really are, not just as they seem to be. Truth has to be penetrated and this journey continues until one reaches the ultimate truth of their entire mental and physical being. When one experiences this truth they learn to stop reacting blindly and to stop creating corruptions. Naturally the old corruptions gradually are eliminated and one will come out of the negativity to experience joy and happiness.

There are three steps of 'virtue' training that were passed on by Dr. Pai. First, one must abstain from any physical or vocal actions which disrupt the peace and harmony of one's self or others. Therefore, a code of morality is the essential first step of the practice. One must not kill, steal, commit sexual misconduct, tell lies, deceive or consume intoxicants such as drugs or alcohol. By refraining from such action, one allows the mind to quiet down and find it's calm center.

The second step is to develop mastery over our undisciplined mind. Start off by training the mind to remain fixed on a single object. The first target of concentration should be one's own breath. Try to keep one's attention for as long as possible on the respiration patterns. One starts by observing natural respiration as it is, as it comes in, as it goes out. Do not try to alter or regulate the natural breathing patterns; this is not an exercise. Calmness overtakes the mind so that it is no longer overpowered by negative distractions. At the same time, one is concentrating the mind, making it sharp, acute and insightful.

The third step is the one that keeps the first two active and developing. One must practice purifying the mind of negativity and corruption by discovering one's own nature. Experiencing one's own reality by observation of their ever-changing mind and the sensations within. This is the culmination of self-purification by self-observation.

Everyone faces the problem of suffering and anyone can practice Chin Kon Pai Meditation to alleviate their suffering. When one suffers from anger they become agitated, negative, pessimistic and distrustful. This will cause dismay in their relationships and an unhappy life with no peace and joy. This malady is universal and it knows no national boundaries. The remedy must also be an universal one: peace, love, understanding, tolerance with ones self and then with others.

Chin Kon Pai is a good remedy. It teaches a code of living which respects the peace and harmony of others. One will learn to develop control over the mind and one will also develop insight into their own reality, through which it is possible to free the mind of negativities.

We can observe reality as it is by observing our truth inside — we do this by getting to know who we really are at the actual, experiential level. As one practices, one journeys out of the misery of defilements. One will transcend experiences and truth which is beyond mind and matter, beyond time and space, beyond the relativity: the truth of total liberation from all impurities, all suffering. The name given to this ultimate truth is irrelevant; it should be the final goal of us all.

Go deep within yourself and discover who you really are. Search for that beauty and pureness that God blessed us all with. You will be excited when you see the truth and moreover, you will learn and be enlightened by the journey.

Chapter 5 - Mind, Thought, Action

"Truly, wisdom springs from meditation;

without meditation, wisdom wanes;

having known these two paths

of progress and decline,

let one conduct oneself

so that wisdom may increase."

Dhammapada

We Are Who We Are Through Our Life's Lessons

Simo Hilda Guerrero Wilson

---

1. **Your body is your shell during this journey.**

You may like it or dislike it, but it is yours for this time around, love it, feel free in it.

2. **Learn Your Lessons.**

You are enrolled in the school of life. Every day you will have a chance to learn lessons. You will come to like the lessons or feel they are irrelevant. Yet they are your schooling.

3. **A flourishing lesson is replicated until learned.**

Our lessons will be offered to us in a mixture of forms. We will eventually learn them. Only then may you go on to the next lesson at hand.

4. **Do not see them as mistakes, they are truly Lessons to learn.**

Development is a process of trial and error: experimentation. The "futile" experiments are just as much part of the process as the experiment that you deem successful.

5. **Learning our lessons never ends.**

Every part of life will contain its lessons. As long as you are living, there will be lessons to learn.

6. **All those around you are merely a mirror of self.**

You will love, hate, like or dislike something about others. It reflects something you love, hate, like or dislike about yourself. We see the world as we are.

7. **There is here and here will be there.**

When you are there it will become here for you, you will simply attain another there that will ultimately look like and become your here. Enlightenment lies in the journey from here to there.

8. **What you become in life is what you choose for yourself to be.**

Every tool and resource you need lies within yourself and being. You now will decide what you do with what you have and are, it is truly your choice and only yours.

9. **All of your answers to all of your questions are already inside you.**

Life's questions are already solved and answered inside you. You need only to look inside yourself. Then trust what you see and feel, it is who you are and what will be.

Lotus Meditation Stances

Full Lotus

Half Lotus

Quarter Lotus

Open Lotus

Chapter 6

Four Supreme States

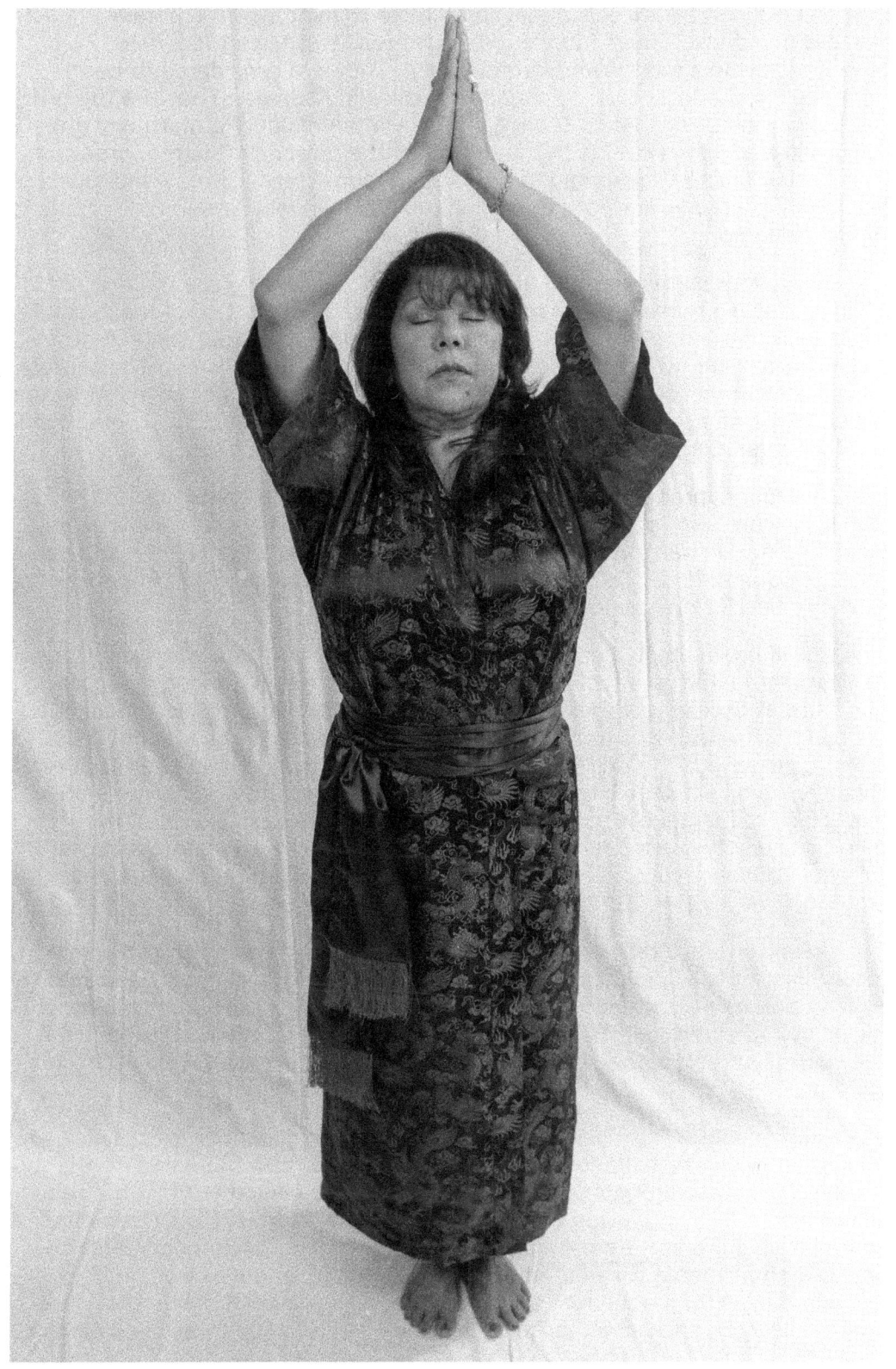

In Chin Kon Pai we talk about four states of mind which embrace our boundless emotions. These four "supreme states" are: loving-kindness, compassion, sympathetic joy and equanimity. They are considered to be the ideal modes of conduct towards society and all living beings. They are the great healers of social tension and variance. They are the builders of harmony and cooperation and they serve as the antidotes to the poisons of hatred, cruelty and envy that are so widespread in our modern subsistence. Study and embrace these four supercilious states, experience them individually and in their subtle yet complex existence.

These four states are said to be sublime because they are the right or ideal way of conducting ourselves towards living beings. The practice of these states provide us with the answers to all challenges arising from social contact. They will remove tension, worry, stress and anxiety from our daily lives. They surely are the immense peace-makers in social conflict, and the great healers of wounds suffered in the struggle of man's existence. They will level social barriers, build congruent communities, and promote humanity against egotism.

The four supreme states - love, compassion, sympathetic joy and equanimity - are also known as the ceaseless states because, in their true nature, they should not be narrowed by any limitation as to the range of beings towards whom they are extended. The states should be non-exclusive and impartial, not bound by selective preferences or prejudices.

It will undoubtedly not be easy for us to apply that boundless application by a deliberate effort and to avoid displaying a degree of partiality. In most cases, we will have to use these four qualities not only as principles of conduct and objects of reflection, but also as subjects of meticulous meditation. That meditation is called Chin Kon Pai, the meditative maturity of the awe-inspiring states. The practical aim is to achieve, with the help of these supreme states, a high stage of mental concentration called "meditative immersion." The meditations on love, compassion and sympathetic joy may each produce the attainment of the first three absorptions, while the meditation on equanimity will lead to the fourth, in which equanimity is the most significant factor.

Persistent meditative practice in Chin Kon Pai will have two substantial effects. First, it will help these four traits sink deep into one's heart and soul so that they posses a spontaneous attitude not easily jaded; second, it will secure their unlimited extension. If Chin Kon Pai is studied correctly and diligently, it will systematically break down all barriers restricting their application to particular individuals.

In meditative exercises, the selection of people to whom the thought of compassion or sympathetic joy is directed progresses from the easier to the more difficult. When meditating on loving or kindness, one should start with a thought of one's own well-being, using this as a point of reference. If I wish to be happy and free from suffering, I must truly feel and see myself being happy and free from suffering. I must wish for all beings to be happy and free from suffering! Then one may extend a thought of loving-kindness to a person who they have a loving respect for, such as a teacher, mentor or leader; then to beloved people, to apathetic ones, and finally to ones they dislike or even enemies. This type of meditational exercise should be aimed only at those who are living.

The same principles of practice apply to the meditative development of compassion, sympathetic joy and equanimity, with variations in the selection of people. The ultimate aim is to produce a state of mind that can serve as a firm basis for developing insight into our true nature. A mind that has achieved meditative assimilation will be pure, tranquil, firm and free of selfishness. It will be well prepared for the final work of deliverance which can be completed only by insight.

Chin Kon Pai meditative practice will help love, compassion, joy and equanimity to become spontaneous. It will help make the mind firmer and calmer in withstanding the numerous irritations in life that challenge us to maintain these four qualities in thoughts, words and deeds. This state of mind will become the norm for the practitioner and with constant and diligent practice it becomes easier and easier. The mind will harbor less resentment, tension and irritability. Our everyday life and thought has a strong influence on the meditative mind; only if the gap between them is tirelessly narrowed will there be a chance for steady meditative progress and for achieving the highest aim of our practice.

Contemplations on the Four Supreme States

LOVE

Love, without desire to possess, knowing well that in the ultimate sense there is no possession and no possessor: this is the highest love.

Love, without speaking and thinking of "I," knowing well that this so-called "I" is a mere delusion.

Love, without selecting and excluding, knowing well that to do so means to create love's own contrasts: dislike, aversion and hatred.

Love, embracing all beings: small and great, far and near, be it on earth, in the water or in the air.

Love, embracing impartially all sentient beings, and not only those who are useful, pleasing or amusing to us.

Love, embracing all beings, be they noble-minded or low-minded, good or evil. The noble and the good are embraced because Love is flowing to them spontaneously. The low-minded and evil-minded are included because they are those who are most in need of Love. In many of them the seed of goodness may have died merely because warmth was lacking for its growth, because it perished from cold in a loveless world.

Love, embracing all beings, knowing well that we all are fellow wayfarers through this round of existence -- that we all are overcome by the same law of suffering.

Love, but not the sensuous fire that burns, scorches and tortures, that inflicts more wounds than it cures -- flaring up now, at the next moment being extinguished, leaving behind more coldness and loneliness than was felt before. Rather, Love that lies like a soft but firm hand on the ailing beings, ever unchanged in its sympathy, without wavering, unconcerned with any response it meets. Love that is comforting coolness to those who burn with the fire of suffering and passion; that is life-giving warmth to those abandoned in the cold desert of loneliness, to those who are shivering in the frost of a loveless world; to those whose hearts have become as if empty and dry by the repeated calls for help, by deepest despair.

Love, that is a sublime nobility of heart and intellect which knows, understands and is ready to help.

Love, that is strength and gives strength: this is the highest Love.

Love, which by the Enlightened One was named "the liberation of the heart," "the most sublime beauty": this is the highest Love.

COMPASSION

The world suffers, while most people have their eyes and ears closed. They do not hear the cry of distress continually pervading the world. Their own grief or joy distorts their sight and deafens their ears. Bound by selfishness, their hearts turn hard and tapered. How may they strive for any higher goal, to realize that only liberation from selfish craving will affect their own release from suffering?

Beings, sunk in ignorance and lost in delusion, one state of suffering to another, not knowing ones real purpose. This insight into the general commandment of suffering is the real foundation of our compassion, not any isolated fact of suffering.

The compassion of a wise man will not render him a victim of suffering. His thoughts, words and deeds are plenty and defined. One's heart must not waver; it must be and remain serene and calm. How else should he be able to help family friends and community?

So we must strive to have compassion arise in our hearts! Compassion that is sublime in one's heart and a developed intellect which knows, understands and is ready to help. With this we can rise above all other and find peace for ourself and others that we touch.

Compassion that is strength and gives strength is the highest form and achievement of compassion. Through Chin Kon Pai meditation we will truly find our strength of compassion.

SYMPATHETIC JOY

Your life will gain in joy by sharing the happiness with others. Our features change and become bright with joy when we are happy. Can joy raise us to noble aspirations and deeds, exceeding their normal capacity? Can a joyful experience fill your own heart with joyful bliss? It is truly in your power to create such an experience of sympathetic joy, by producing happiness in oneself and others, by fostering joy and solace.

Noble and sublime joy is not foreign to the Teachers, leaders and Enlightened people of our world. Our teachings show us the path that leads us step by step to an ever purer and loftier happiness.

Noble and sublime joy will be a colleague on the path to the extermination of suffering and distress. One who is possessed with joy finds that serene calmness leading to a contemplative state of mind. And only a mind serene and collected is able to gain the liberating wisdom. The wisdom that will make us better people and leaders. We must help others to find the divine path and the way.

EQUANIMITY

Equanimity is the perfect, unshakable balance of one's mind that is rooted in our insight. Looking at the world around us, and looking into our own heart, we see clearly how difficult it is to attain and sustain balance of one's mind.

Looking into life we notice how it repetitively moves between contrasts: rise and fall, success and failure, loss and gain, honor and guilt. We feel how our heart responds to all this with happiness and sorrow, disappointment and satisfaction, hope and fear. These waves of emotion carry us up and throw us down and no sooner do we begin to rest than we are hit with a new wave of emotion and energy.

Equanimity or composure has to be based on a vigilant presence of mind, one cannot have an indifferent lifelessness present in their mind. To attain this state one must practice a deliberate training, it is not the casual outcome of a passing mood. But equanimity would not be present within if it had to be produced by exertion again and again. True equanimity, however, should be able to meet all these severe tests and to regenerate its strength from sources within. It will possess great power of resistance and self-renewal only if it is accompanied by the other three supreme states.

All the various events of our lives are the result of our deeds. Sometimes our actions return to us in the way that others treat us, and that we treat others. Often the results go against our expectations or contrary to what we feel should be the result. Such experiences point out to us consequences of our deeds whether we foresee them or not. If we learn to see things from all angles, and to read the message conveyed by our own experience, then suffering will not be perceived so drastically and we will cope with our lessons more easily. Our experiences will be a stern but truthful companion and a well-meaning one who teaches us the most difficult subject of all: knowledge about ourselves. By looking at suffering as our teacher and companion, we will succeed in enduring it with equanimity. Disgust will arise at our own craving, at our own delusion, at our own propensity to create situations which try our strength, our resistance and our equanimity.

All the various events of our lives, being the result of our deeds, will also be our companion, even if they bring us sorrow and pain. Such experiences point out to us consequences of our deeds we did not foresee; they render visible half-conscious motives of our former actions which we tried to hide even from ourselves, covering them up with various pretexts. If we learn to see things from all angles, and to read the message conveyed by our own experience, then suffering, too, will be our companion.

How, then, do these four supreme states suffuse each other?

Unbounded love guards compassion.

Love imparts to equanimity.

Compassion prevents love and sympathetic joy from forgetting.

Compassion guards equanimity from falling into a cold indifference.

Sympathetic joy holds compassion back from becoming overwhelmed.

Sympathetic joy gives to equanimity the mild serenity that softens its stern appearance.

Equanimity rooted in insight is the guiding and restraining power.

Equanimity is a perfect, unshakable balance of mind.

For one who clings, motion exists; but for one who clings not, there is no motion. Where there is no motion, there is stillness. Where stillness is, there is no craving. Where no craving is, there is neither coming nor going. Where no coming or going is, there is neither arising nor passing away. Where neither arising nor passing away is, there is neither this world nor a world beyond, nor a state between. This, verily, is the end of suffering. Know who you are, be that person and give peace and joy to your life and all those lives that you touch.

Chapter 6 - Four Supreme States

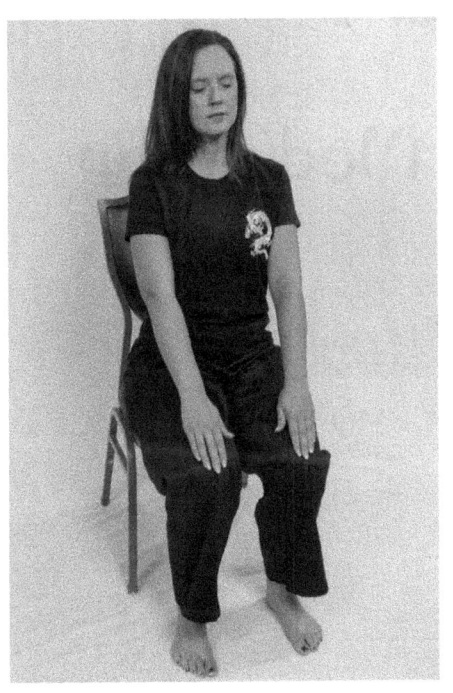
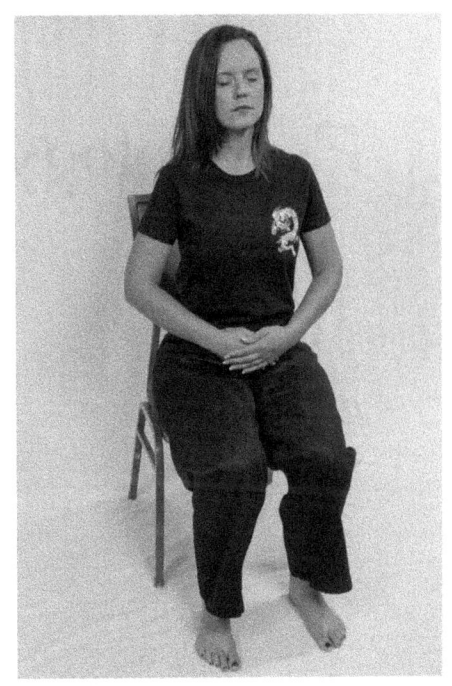

Chapter 7
Psychology of Meditation

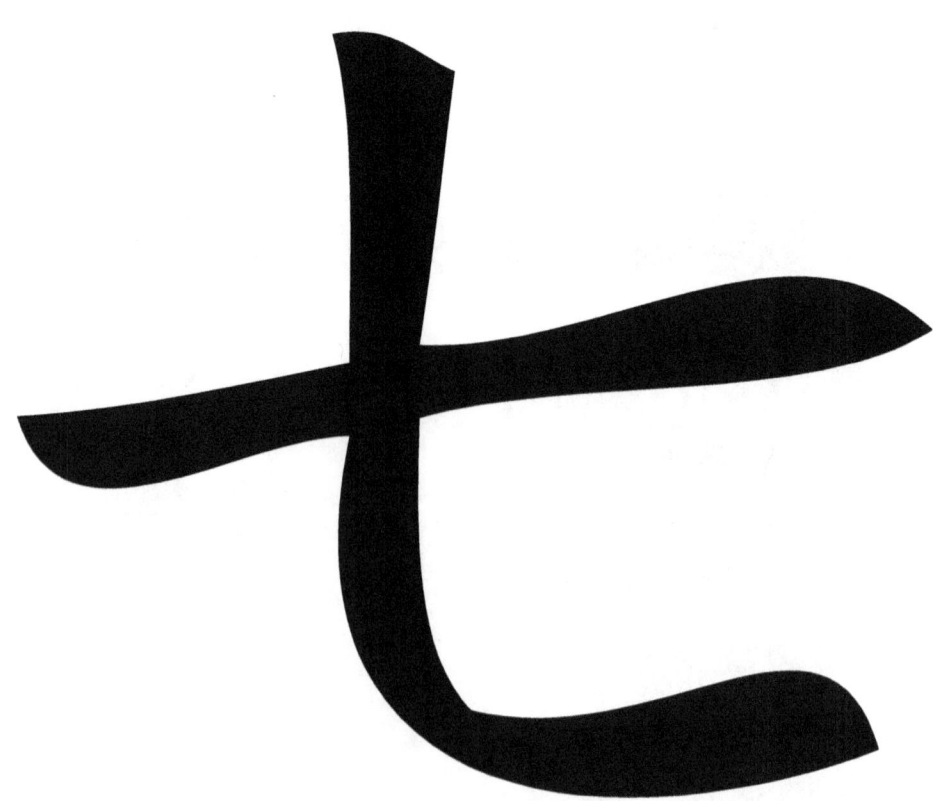

Chapter 7 - Pyschology of Meditation

Why the Psychology of meditation? What does it mean to a practitioner or those contemplating the practice of Chin Kon Pai Meditation? Throughout the world today and for centuries people look at life differently. Rather it be the highlands of Tibet, China, Japan, the vast lands of Russia, the centuries old regions of Scotland, Ireland, France or Germany, the ancient civilizations of Africa or the western regions of North America, Central America and the immense land mass of South America, people live and often think differently. There are influences of cultural backgrounds, big city or remote wildernesses, social experiences of peace or war as well as interaction with other types of people. These are just a few of the variables that make us different.

Yet with so many criteria that make so many people different there is always one common bond: our minds. Our thought process works the same and we have established thoughts and opinions that may stay the same and may be altered. These alterations may come by the words or actions of others or by our own choice. This is truly the most powerful action on mother earth, the power to change thought and then action by our own will at any time we choose.

So how do different societies deal with challenges better and with a greater sense of calmness and why does it seem that some societies of people can deal with adversities, challenges and threat better than others? This is to say, not as an individual person making an individual thought and decision, but as a social group. The answer lies in the thought process of a group that is set by a culture and its way of perceiving events around them. When we think through a situation we are influenced by many things, some consciously and some subconsciously.

There are many places on earth where the people live with very little on a monetary standard. They do not have expensive homes, make big annual salaries, drive fancy automobiles or have all the luxuries that their hearts desire. Yet these people are very happy, at peace with themselves and their neighbors, and look forward to a happy and meaningful life for them and their families. So are we to accept as true that we do not need all of the things that we are programmed to believe we must have to be happy? And why are some people happy while possessing many items of value and leading a successful lifestyle by the standards of their society? It all goes back to what is in our mind and how we exercise our mind to think and perceive life around us that is the essence of Chin Kon Pai meditation. The psychology of it all is to know why our meditation makes us think the way we do, it is all our choice to understand or reject. It is recognizing our own inner calm; recognize it and you can cultivate it.

So by making the personal choice to recognize our own 'place of inner calmness' we open up a whole thought process to finding inner peace whenever we wish by practicing our meditation. We can find a tranquil state and utilize it to make decisions that will determine our approach to life. Blending these philosophies into ones daily life is very foreign to most people and especially our busy, fast paced, high achieving western lifestyle. It has become unfamiliar to us and what is unfamiliar becomes harder to recognize. What becomes difficult to recognize seems harder to achieve and if we can not achieve a level of inner peace we will be sickened by the unrest. This unrest can be the very cause of our social disease!

If we indeed want to be better as a person and collectively as a society, what do we do? Well, there is no need to quit your job, give away all of your possessions, throw on a robe and move to the top of a mountain in total seclusion. Make the choice to travel the path to find your 'place of inner calmness.' Research indicates that with just a few minutes a day of meditation one may dramatically begin to change their lives in a positive fashion. By just a little practice one can increase their Alpha Waves 'relaxed brain waves' which will in turn decrease stress, anxiety, depression and negative feelings. Imagine what an increased and heightened level of meditation will do for us as individuals and for our communities as a social group. It really is a personal choice that has no limitations on what a person can achieve and the mental level of calmness they will posses.

The practice of meditation will activate parts of the brain that are responsible for the autonomic nervous system. This will directly affect the different functions in our body that we do not have direct control over such as the cardio vascular system and digestive system. These functions are often compromised by negativity, stress and anxiety. If one allows these harmful emotions to persist for a prolonged amount of time digestive problems, heart disease and infertility may be created or agitated.

So how does one practice and achieve a polymorphous nature by psychologically and physiologically practicing this exercise we know as meditation? With all of the distractions around us how do we keep from adding to or subtracting from our heightened essence of peace? It is pretty basic, if you feel the result that you were striving for, peace and tranquility, you are on the correct path. It truly is an individual journey, no two are the same and no two journeys will have the same result.

One of the greatest psychological challenges and obstacles when practicing meditation can be what we call 'internal disturbance of chatter.' One must start off with baby steps on their meditation path. Too much, too soon can divert from the relaxation path and a person will concentrate on their anxiety and the very reasons that they came to meditation in the first place. By finding ones own 'place of inner calmness' the practitioner will begin with small progressions to calm themselves and concentrate on a positive force. This is proven to cultivate self acceptance and facilitate a better state of ones mental health and self consciousness.

Keep in mind that a better awareness of self may be a proverbial double edge sword. One of the ironies of getting to know your thoughts and finding who you are is to be met with the challenge of owning up to yourself. This is why it should be done in short stages and with the greatest direction of positive and peaceful intent at all times. Keep in mind that the misconception of baring or emptying the mind is NOT what meditation is at all. You never truly can rid your own thoughts; you categorize them, comprehend them, systematize your intent and peacefully assemble your 'state of mind.'

Rather it be psychotherapy or meditation one does not want to struggle with the preoccupation of their thought but they should strive to find peace with their now existence. With Chin Kon Pai meditation we learn that there is very little difference between psychoanalytical theories and our basic individual experiences. Our nature is simplistic and natural to the ways of life. So we must strive to journey the path of simple pure thought with the understanding that nothing is lasting or separate from itself.

As we touched on earlier the practice of meditation has a cross over affect between the psychological and the physiological effects on the practitioner. Research in the last two decades has shown that the effects of meditation certainly do calm the mind, decrease anxiety and minimize our stress levels. We now believe that the interaction between the mental and physical effects certainly is profound. It is widely believed that a regular meditation program may reverse heart disease, decrease the risk of heart attack or stroke, reduce pain and enhance one's natural immune system. One may find themselves with more energy, less confusion in their daily life, better digestion, less gastrointestinal challenges and just a better overall feeling in their wonderful body.

So we ask ourselves how this all takes place. What is the mystery of a meditation healing? What Psychologist, Medical Doctors and Meditation Masters have all agreed on is that a good and continuous meditation practice reduces the stress hormone cortisol. It is really easy to understand. Reduce stress in your life, control as much of the stress that you do maintain and you will send a message to the rest of the body that you are healthier and in better control of your self.

So now we understand the correlation between the mental and physical benefits of a regular practice of meditation, why doesn't everyone just do it? Misconceptions of what meditation really is have been a great part of resistance to the practice. Also, many of our societies believe in the quick fix from outside sources, even if they are not long term. The practice of meditation will place one in the middle of their existence and they will clearly see who they are and what affects they have on themselves as well as others. For some that may be uncomfortable, even though that may be just what they need.

Ones own ego, fear, mental stability and internal challenges may steer them away from taking a good look at themselves. If they have trouble focusing on their own being, look slightly away from the light and they may focus easier and have a clearer picture of themselves as well as others. Detach from the ego and stress, this is the start of a great journey of awareness and soon to be peace.

Chapter 7 - Pyschology of Meditation

Other Seated Meditation Stances

Diamond

Chapter 7 - Pyschology of Meditation

Warrior

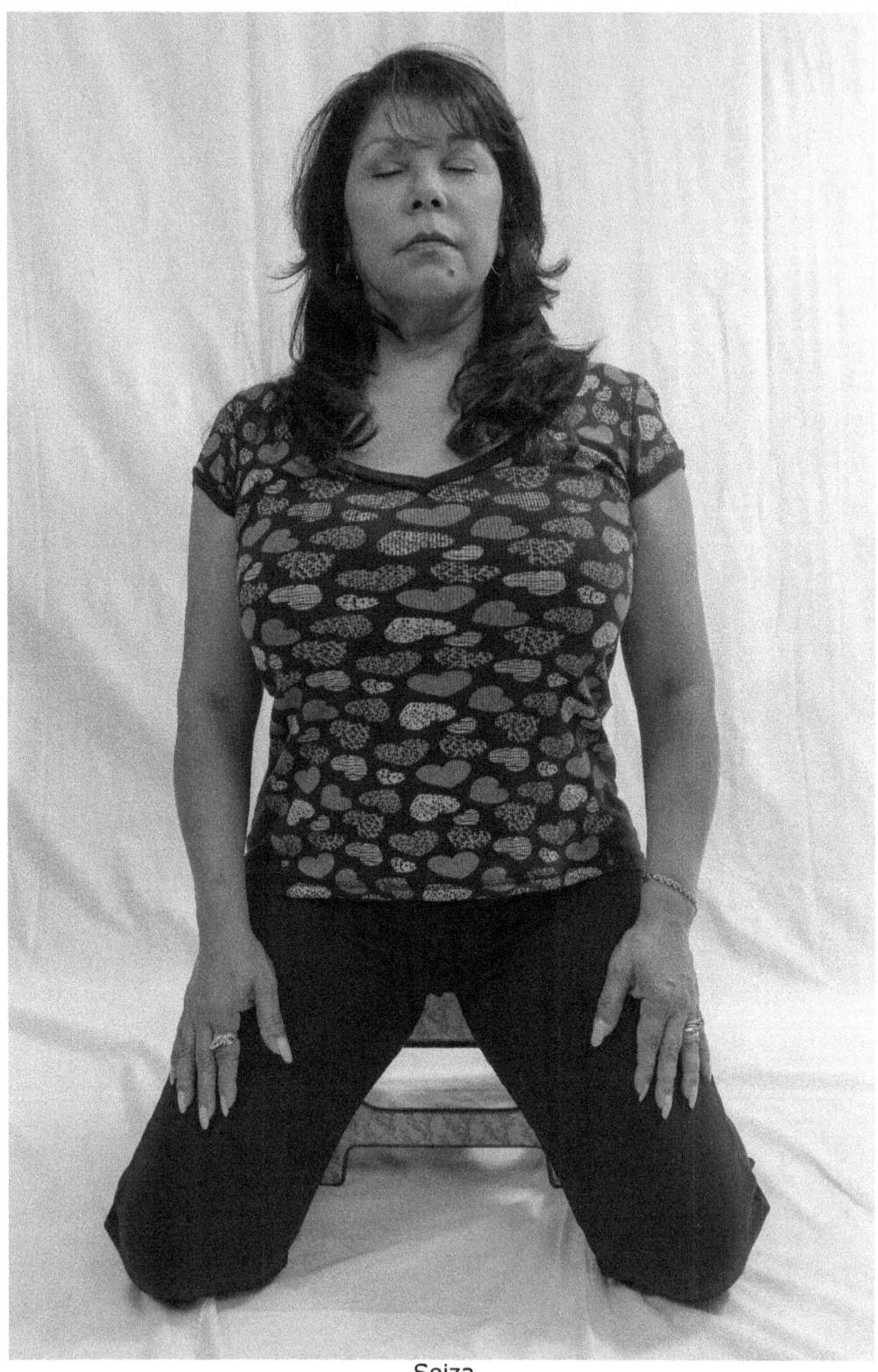

Seiza

Chapter 7 - Pyschology of Meditation

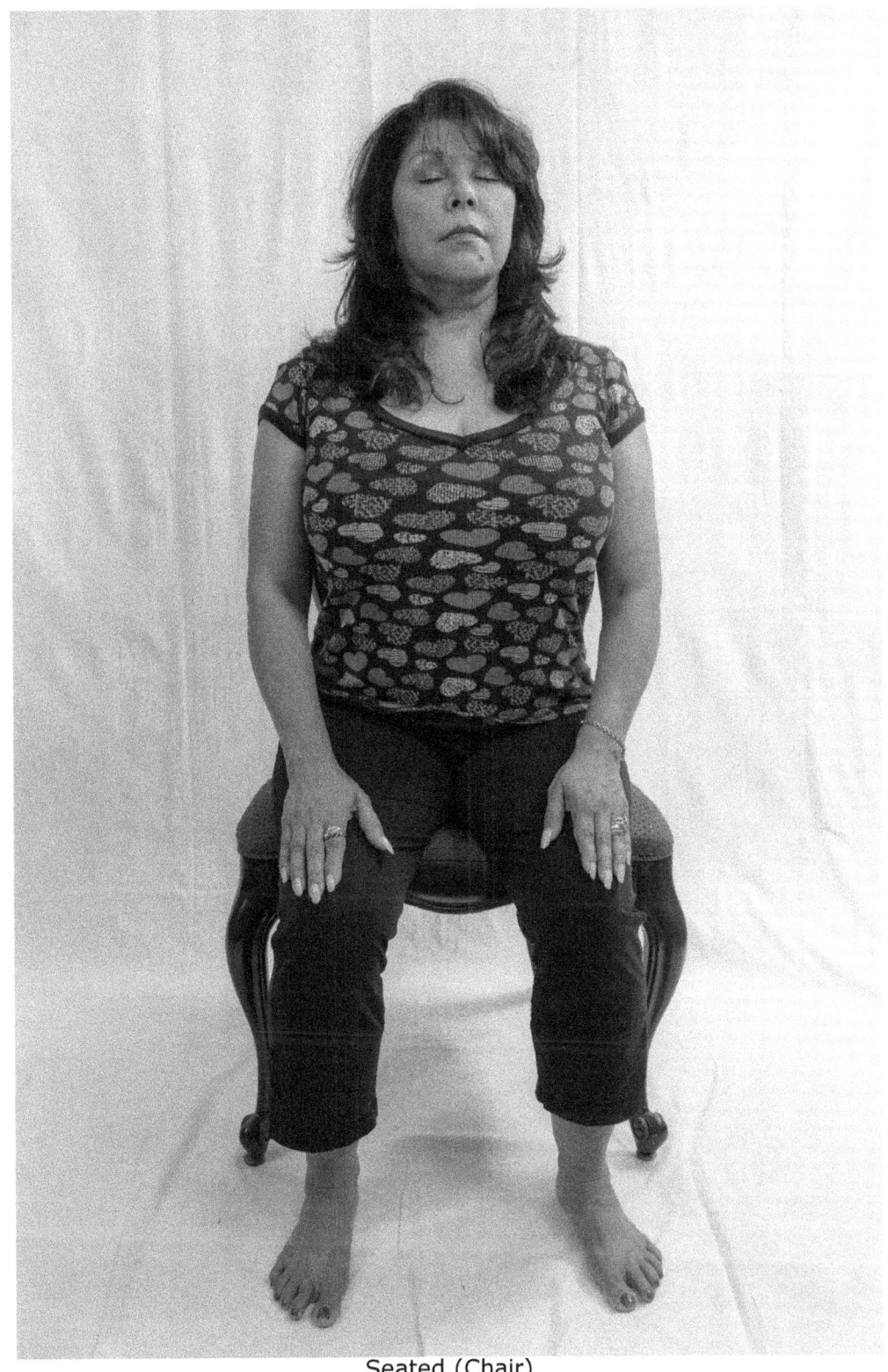

Seated (Chair)

Chapter 8

Find Your Rest

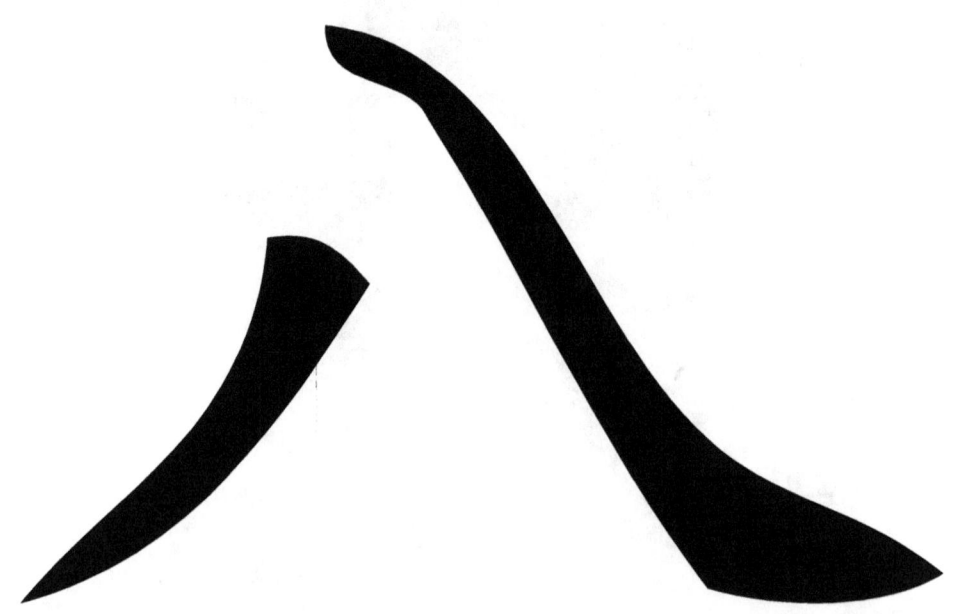

When the mind becomes quiet, mental stillness is created. By bringing the body, mind, and senses into balance, in turn, relaxes the nervous system. When we are grounded physically and mentally, we are keenly aware of our senses, yet disengaged at the same time.

By dictionary definition, "meditation" means to reflect upon, ponder, or contemplate. It can also signify a devoted exercise of contemplation or a contemplative discourse of a religious or philosophical nature. The word meditate comes from the Latin meditari, which means to think about or consider. Med is the root of this word and means "to take appropriate measures." In our culture, to meditate can be interpreted several ways.

Wandering thoughts is perhaps the greatest challenge for us. What do we do when we begin thinking during meditation? First, we bring our attention back to our posture and breathing, giving our full attention fully to them. This means a straighter spine, including the small of the back curved slightly in, is the neck long, is my chin pushing forward. Remember you can also have your thinking count the breaths, say on the exhalation, or note the breath as it proceeds in and out.

The second strategy involves giving your thinking a task. For instance, you could challenge your thinking with specific questions, such as, "What is it you really want?" or "What is the most important point?". Any one of these activities can keep thinking occupied. In a sense, what you are doing is inviting your thinking to join you in meditation rather than trying to exclude it. Always be mindful that you and your thoughts are aiming to discover creative, enjoyable ways to meditate—as well as ways to live, awaken, and benefit each other. Think of your thinking not as an adversary but as a spiritual friend.

Let us be still for a few moments

Without moving even our little finger

So that a hush descends upon us.

There would be no place to go,

Nor to come from,

For we would have arrived in this extraordinary moment

There would be a stillness and silence,

That would fill all of our senses,

Where all things would find their rest.

Everything would then be together in a deep connection.

Putting an end to "us and them", this against that.

> We would not move in these brief moments
>
> For that would disturb this palpable presence;
>
> There would be nothing to be said nor done
>
> For life would embrace us in this wondrous meeting
>
> And take us into its arms as a loving friend.
>
> There would be a stillness and silence,
>
> That would fill all of our senses,
>
> Where all things would find their rest.
>
> Everything would then be together in a deep connection.
>
> Putting an end to "us and them", this against that.
>
> We would not move in these brief moments
>
> For that would disturb this palpable presence;
>
> There would be nothing to be said nor done
>
> For life would embrace us in this wondrous meeting
>
> And take us into its arms as a loving friend.

There are many things in life that are beyond our control. However, it is possible to take responsibility for and to change one's state of mind. In Chin Kon Pai meditation this is the most important thing we can do. We are taught that it is a great antidote to the anxiety, hatred, discontentedness, stress, and confusion that overwhelms the human condition.

Chin Kon Pai meditation can be a means of transforming the mind. Its practices are techniques that foster a positive environment and develop concentration and clarity. By engaging in meditation one learns the patterns and habits of the mind, and the practice offers a means to cultivate new, more positive ways of being. With persistence and patience these calm and focused states of mind can deepen into profoundly tranquil and energized states of mind. Such experiences can have a transformational effect and can lead to a new understanding and appreciation of our lives.

Make Chin Kon Pai a part of your daily existence. Great Grandmaster - Dr. Daniel Kane Pai taught that a man cannot be whole without an understanding of self. That self is what lies within us; it is not our external shell. Breathe like a baby, think with the innocence of a child and make sound decisions of a mature adult. Live everyday with a positive state of mind and being. Be blessed and spread Peace & Joy to all those you encounter.

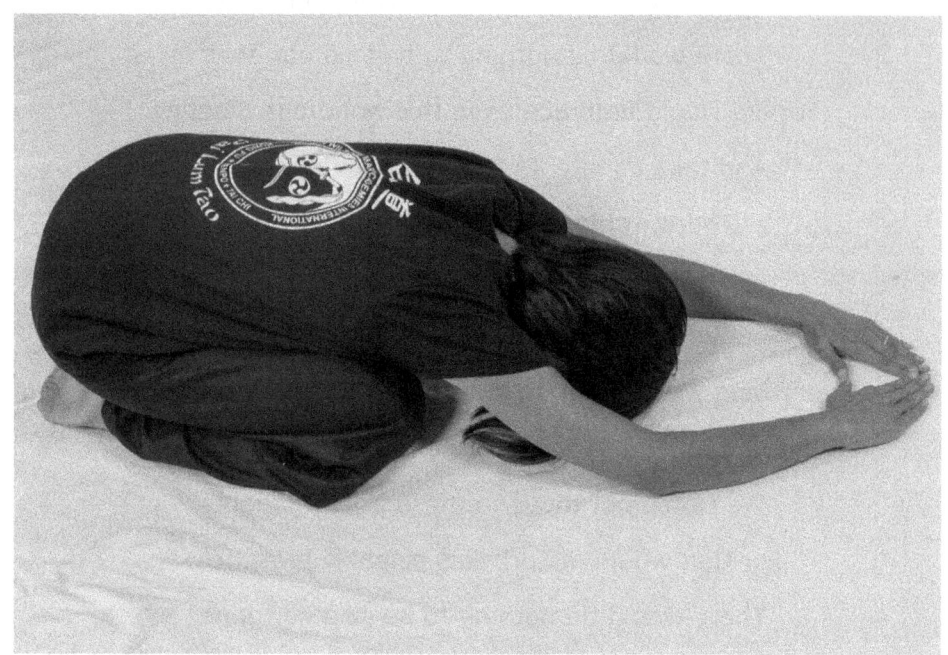

Chapter 8 - Find your Rest

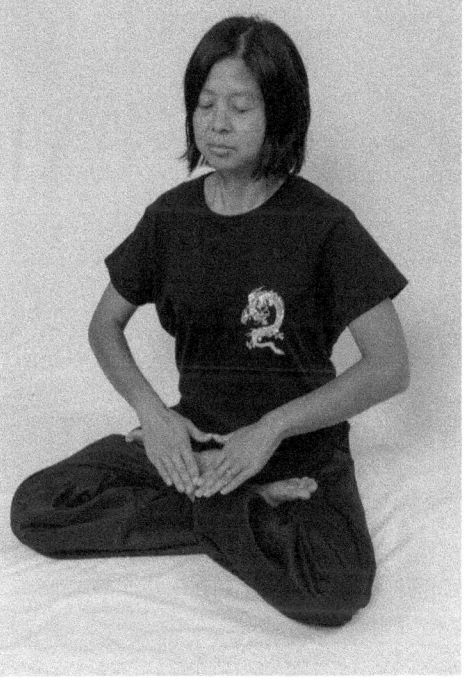

Lying Meditation Postures

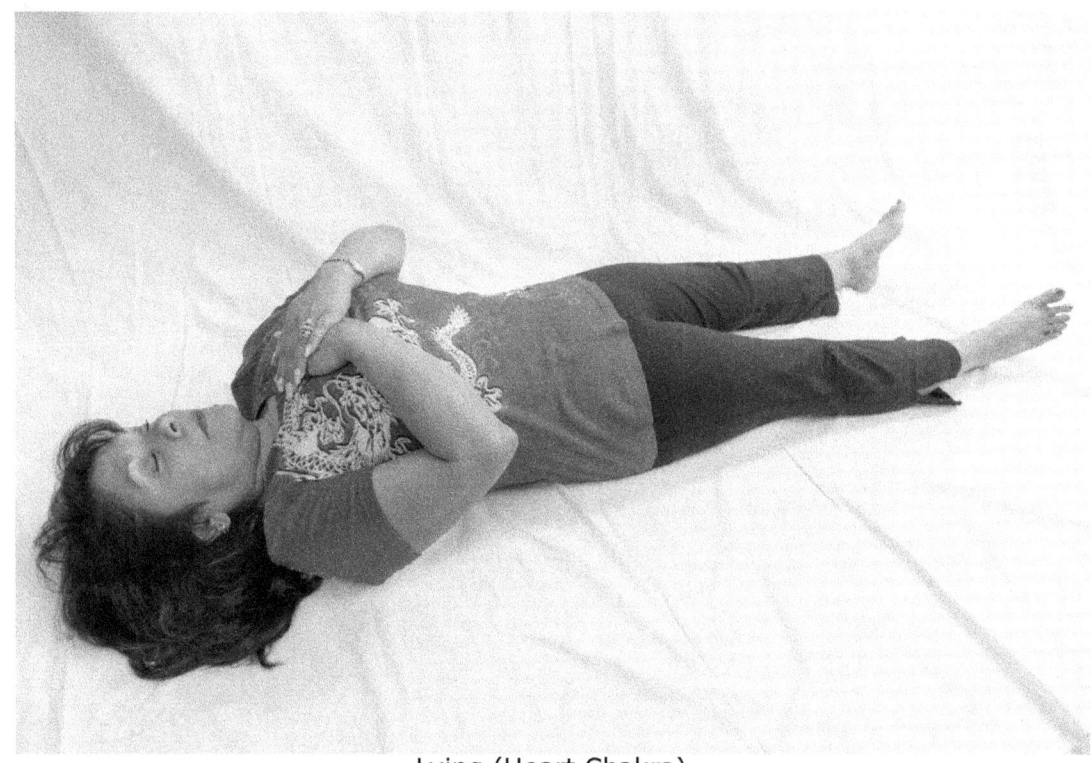

Lying (Heart Chakra)

Chapter 8 - Find your Rest

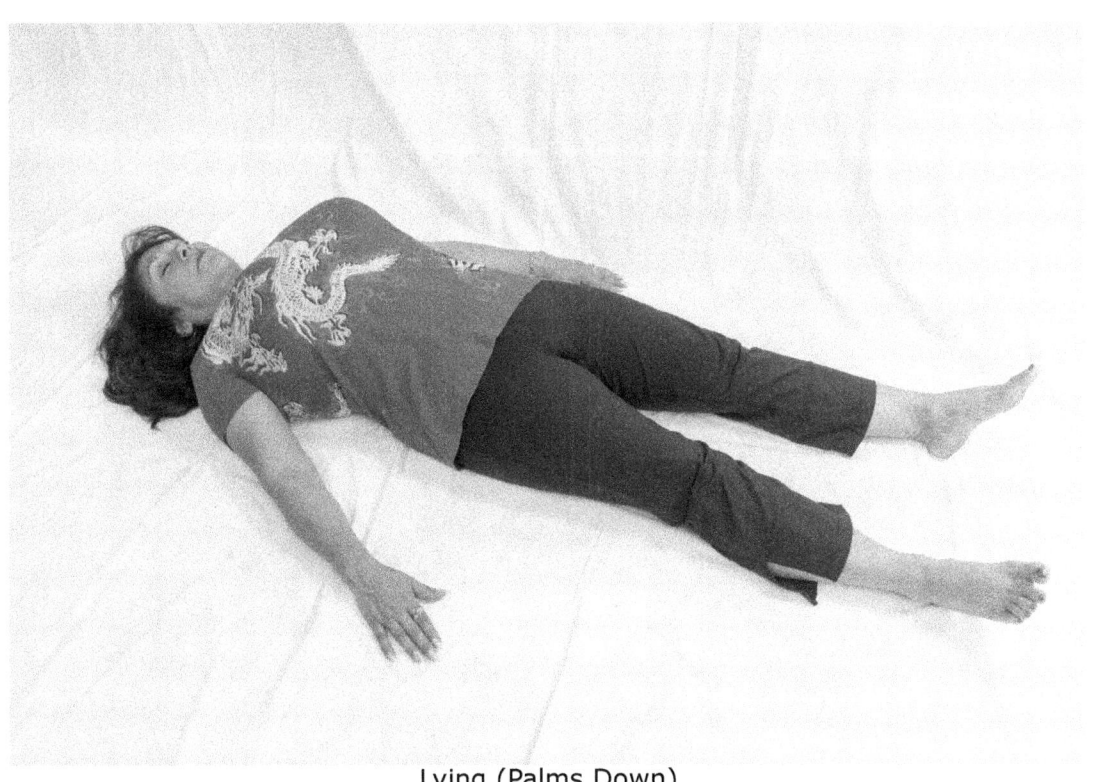

Lying (Palms Down)

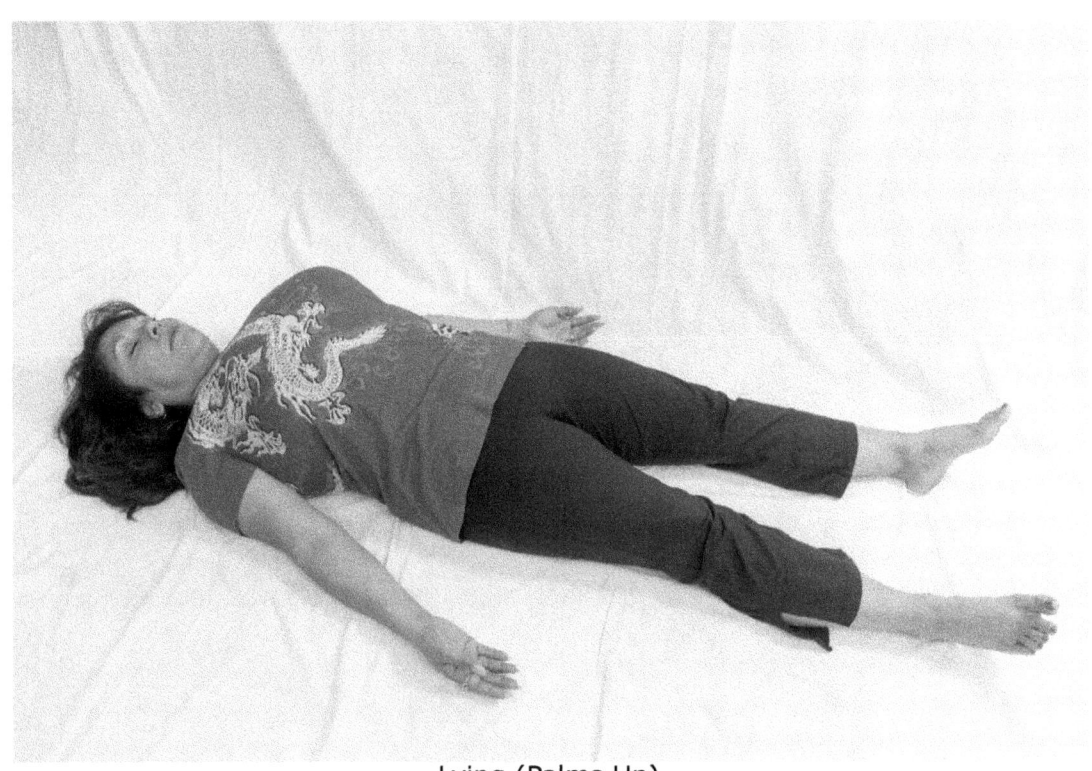
Lying (Palms Up)

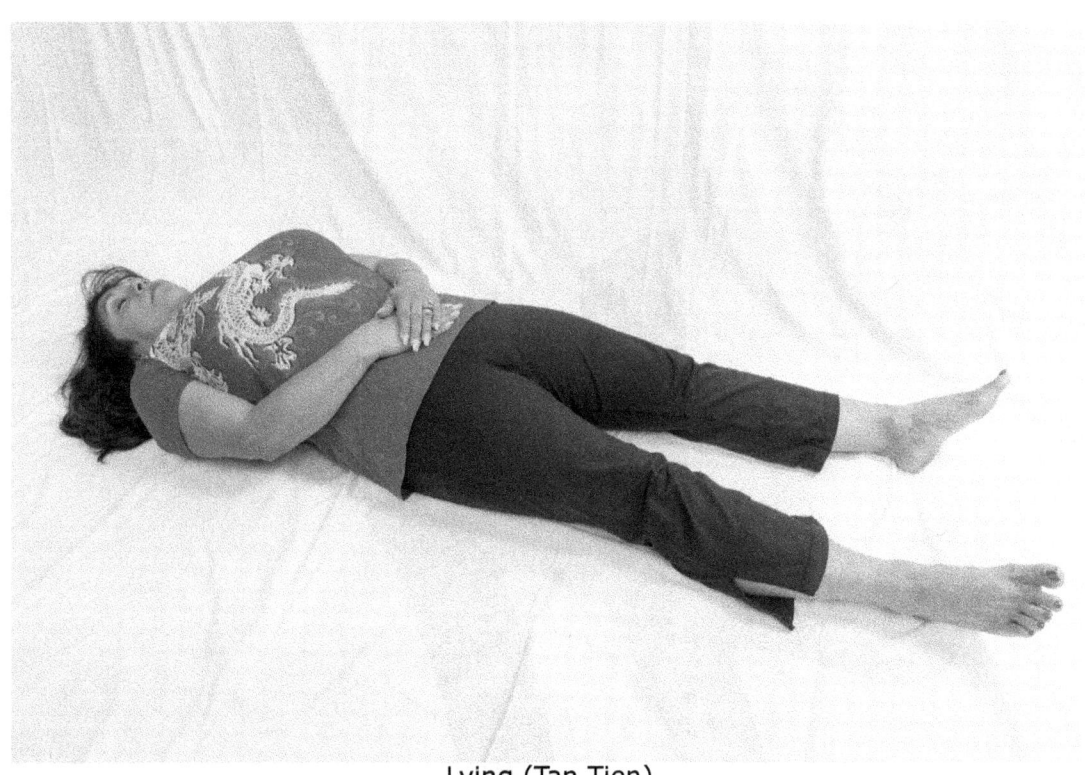

Lying (Tan Tien)

Chapter 9

Chi Development Through Meditation

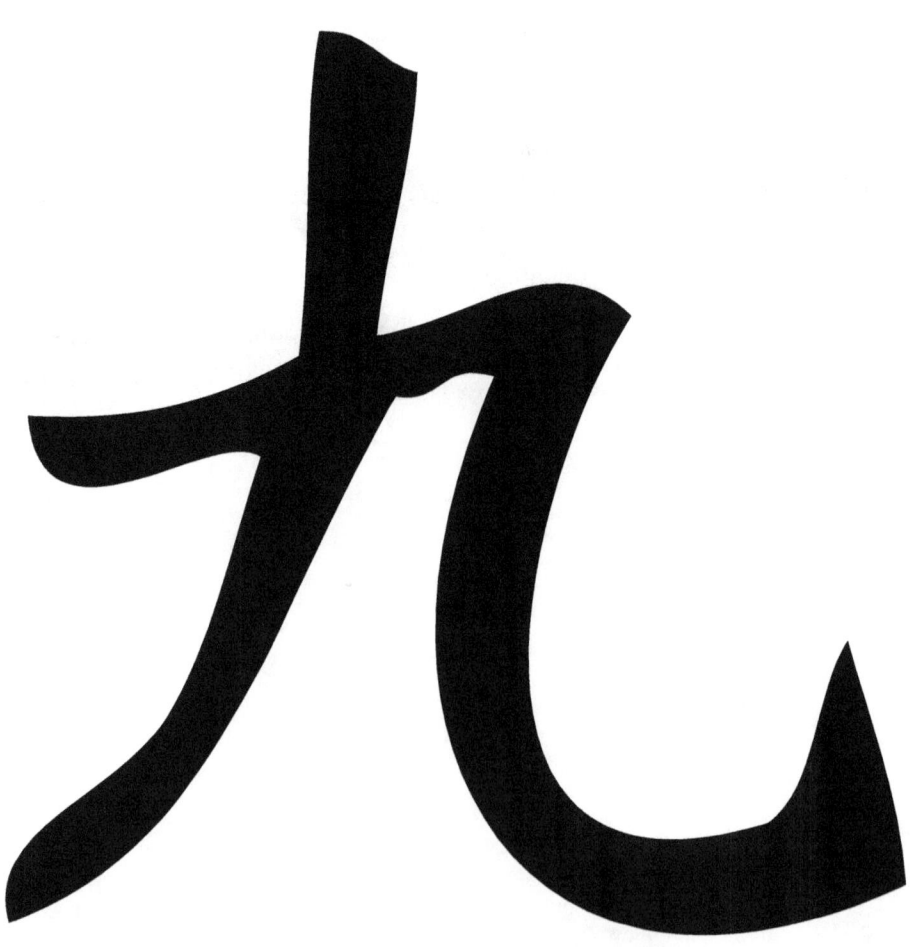

The improvement of Chi, your life energy, can be developed with meditation. To start you need to know that there are many forms of meditation. The static or unmoving meditations that consist of standing, sitting or laying meditations are the more popular styles of meditations. The next kind of meditation would be active or moving meditation. This style of meditation normally takes a bit more focus and physical discipline from the practitioner. There is also the guided meditation, a very useful and effective way to develop and practice meditation. Through these styles of meditation your Chi development will be transformed to a stronger and more productive use of your life energy.

One of the most common types of meditation that people know about would be the static or unmoving meditation. This kind of meditation has the user in a seated, laying or standing position without any movement. Without having any movement you are able to learn how to let the body relax and let the mind become more aware and in touch with one's self. Once you have gotten to this point of awareness, you can then start to focus on different parts of your body to develop and move Chi to where you are focusing on in the body. There are two ways that you can have your focus to bring energy to the area.

The first is bringing Chi to the point of focus, which would be an internal focus of utilizing your own energy already within the body. This use of Chi would be a masculine, Yang use of energy. By using energy already within the body you will feel the body become much warmer in this area and possibly even see a reddening of the skin from all the blood being pulled to the area. Now the Chi can start to be moved from this area to other parts of the body with more ease, since the Chi has already been pulled into one location. One main factor that contributes to bringing and moving the Chi would be your breath. When moving Chi to a specific location you will need the use of an exhale. The exhale will not only help with the mental aspect of moving the Chi, but also help with the relaxation of the body to allow movement of energy. The use of using your own internal energy can have the side effect of tiring the body and mind.

The second form of directing Chi would be an external focus of pulling the energy into the body. This is the female, Yin aspect of pulling Chi into the body. Drawing energy into the body instead of using the energy already within the body will cause a cooling sensation in the area. The more Chi that you can pull in at one time will result in the area becoming colder. The use of breath is also important; by inhaling you are naturally pulling energy into the body and by having your focus on a specific area the Chi will be more concentrated to that spot. With the use of drawing energy into the body, you will also need to have a way of expelling the excess energy when you are finished. If you do not get rid of the excess Chi then you may have other complications, such as insomnia.

The best effect would be to combine both the female (Yin) and male (Yang) aspects of energy work. Using the female aspect of drawing the energy into the body and then, since the energy is already within the body, now utilize the male aspect of energy work and push it to the areas in need. Just with one complete breath you can start to achieve more results than the use of male or female energy work separately. Yin is also considered as the mental body and Yang is considered as the physical body. Only when both Yin and Yang are in harmony can you have good health. There will be times that you will need to focus more on one aspect than the other to get the balance point of Yin and Yang.

Other aspects that are tied into the balance of Yin and Yang would be Can, which is the Chinese word for water, and Lii, which is the Chinese word for fire. Can is a formless form and shapeless shape. Can will help you to develop more Yin. Utilizing Can in your meditation will help you develop more Yin Chi. Can is considered as the essence of life and by using Can, you will be able revitalize the body and mind. Lii is considered a destructive force and it will help you to develop more Yang. Utilizing Lii in your meditation will help you to develop more Yang Chi. Lii being a destructive force will be used to break down blockages or barriers within the body. This will help to open and clear a path for the body to heal. Can and Lii are the methods or causes to the person. Yin and Yang are the results. Regulating these causes the balance of Yin and Yang.

One of the more effective ways of developing Chi would be with active or moving meditation. This may be the most effective way for development of Chi, but also the most difficult way of meditation. The movements need to be done over and over again until the practitioner is not focused upon the movement any more. The body will start to do the movement on it's own without the thought of the consciousness. This takes quite a bit of practice to get the muscles to relax and know the movements. Once you have gotten to this state then you are able to start the meditative state. Using moving meditation will help you to focus energy into the areas that are moving. It is natural for the energy to be going and being pulled into these areas. Your focus will help gather energy more efficiently. Active meditation can be used to pull energy into certain parts of the body or into the whole body. It can also be used to get rid of any excess energy with the male aspect of energy. The same concept of drawing or pushing energy around the body that is used with static meditation is used with active meditation.

The use of guided meditation is by far one of the easiest methods of starting out your meditations. It can be done in a group or individual setting. There are also many multimedia avenues that are available to the user to be of use in your own home. Having a guide directing your thoughts to get your body and consciousness into a relaxed state is the first step that has to be taken on this journey into one's self. After the guide has gotten his group or individual to this state, he can then through instinct or by what had been prearranged through discussion help to focus the mind and Chi to different parts of the body for healing or for opening up energy channels such as meridians or chakras.

The methods of developing Chi are many and the balance of Chi in the body takes time and patience. Without utilizing the tools to develop and harness Chi, your own physical and mental health become at risk. The body needs to keep itself in harmony. Meditation is a wonderful and powerful way of creating this harmony. Your efforts should be done on a daily basis. Meditation will also guide you into more insight of yourself and the world as well as the development of your Chi.

Chapter 9 - Chi Development Through Meditation   119

Chapter 10

Mind Over Matter

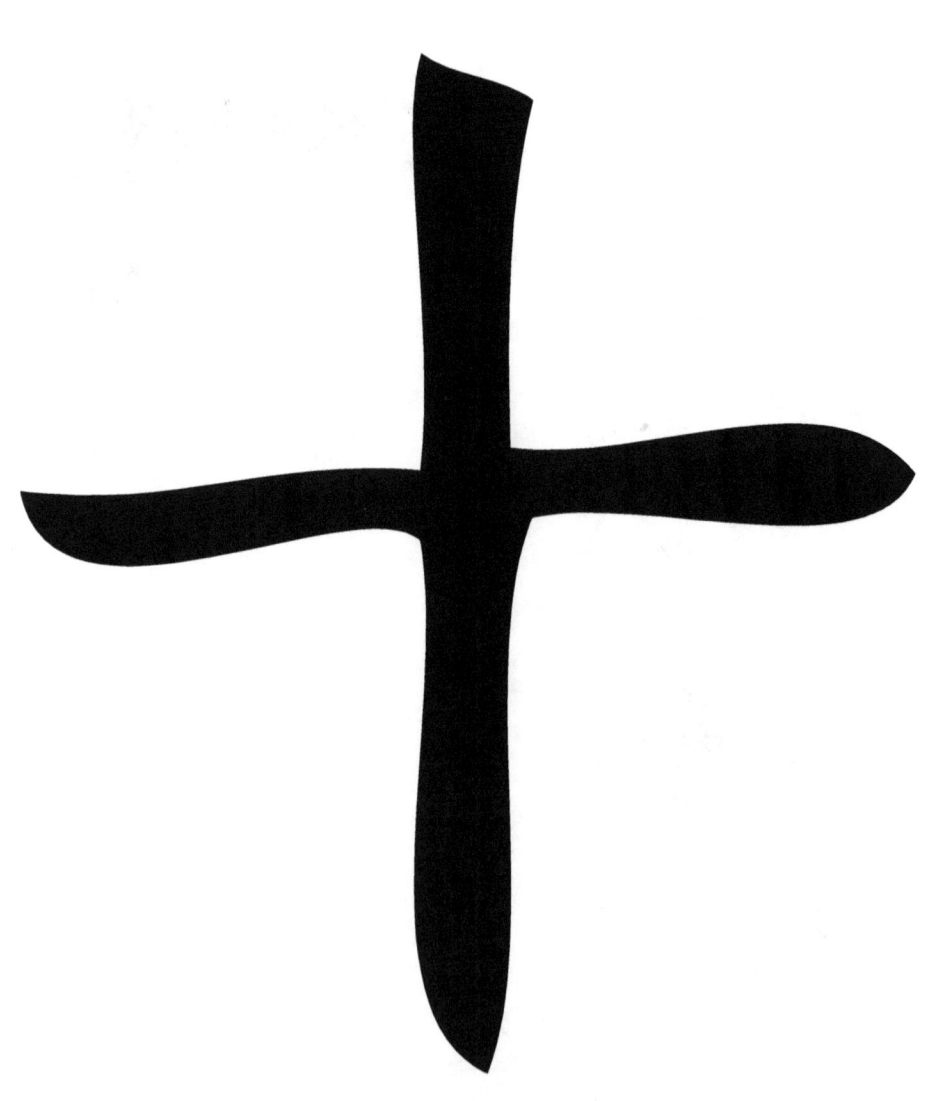

Chapter 10 - Mind Over Matter

In our world today we are hard pressed to go through our day without being bombarded with some kind of stress. Although stress is necessary, too much negative stress is very detrimental to our health. I differentiate hear between positive and negative stress because it is the stress of life that triggers our mind and body to take action. Without these triggers our body's systems would not be and could not work together. Looking at how this works we find another instance where one of the martial arts favorite symbols has a profound significance!

Yin- Yang

Yin - Yang, the balance of all things.

In the context of this discussion, the balance between positive and negative stress in our lives. Yes, I say balance because both are needed for our bodies to function at an optimal level. Some might ask, if negative stress is so bad then shouldn't we try to eliminate it from our lives. This would be nice except for the fact that it is the existence and amount of negative stress that prompts many of our bodies systems into action.

One of the major grouping of actions that our body uses that you may be aware of is what is known as, "The fight or flight response". This group of actions is put into play when we perceive a situation as being a threat. I say perceive here because it is the way that we look at the given set of circumstances that triggers our response. When we perceive something as a threat then our body gets ready to either "fight" or "flee".

At that time the body secretes certain hormones that affect the body in predictable ways. One is Epinephrine and another is Cortisol. In doing this certain actions are started into motion.

Increased heart rate

Increased respiratory rate

Immune system activates

Pupils dilate

Increase in Blood Glucose level

Increased muscle tension.

These are all good and necessary if the situation warrants. That is ones own preservation! The systems operation serves a function that is necessary, but when the situation is resolved it lets the body go into another system, "relaxation"! This system helps restore the homeostasis or balance in the body. That word "balance" - it's everywhere!

What happens if we keep getting bombarded with problems in our everyday lives? Does anyone ever have that happen? Well, if you're anything like me I think you know the answer! Yes!! Let's look at what happens when that "fight or flight" system is forced to work overtime.

Let's for times sake, focus today on one of the hormones secreted during times of stress, Cortisol.

Cortisol is in charge of glucose metabolism, regulation of blood pressure and immune system functions. Prolonged stress keeps Cortisol levels high. This also keeps all the side effects of that at an abnormal level. This is detrimental to the body! Increased blood glucose levels leads to diabetes and the myriad of problems that come with it.

For now let's just focus on the increased Cortisol level and problems.

It has been shown that when these levels remain elevated for a prolonged period many different things can and will happen.

Impaired cognitive performance

Suppressed thyroid function

Hyperglycemia

Decreased bone density

Decrease in muscle tissue

Elevated blood pressure

Lowered Immune levels

Increased abdominal fat

Increased LDL (bad) Cholesterol

Decreased HDL (good) Cholesterol

It is easy to see from this list that it is not good for our bodies! The balance is not there. We need to eliminate the harmful effects. This is where we need to bring our training and knowledge into play.

Meditation is our best countermeasure for the stress we fight every day. It is good for us in many ways. The obvious calming of our minds is only the tip of the proverbial iceberg.

Meditation has been shown to trigger the body into the function of the "relaxation" system. As I said, this system works to bring all the body functions back to a normal balance. When it accomplishes its job our body is back in an environment where it can flourish. I'm sure that this is something that everyone wants, but not something many people think that they have so much control over.

The importance of taking the time for ourself is greater now than ever. Giving ourselves the choice to take control of the course of our health is important. If I may paraphrase here, "I am what I am because I choose to be!"

Chapter 10 - Mind Over Matter 125

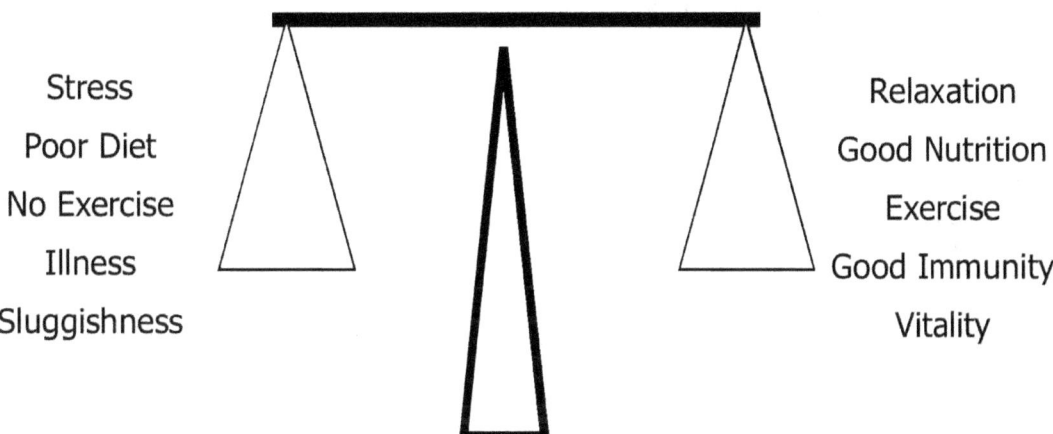

This says it all! We, for our own sake, should choose to take the path that will be in our own best interest!

The type of meditation that we choose is not as important as the fact that we do it!

As long as the quality of the time spent meditating is good, the type is not of major importance. Don't get caught up in the pitfalls of "it has to be this position or this time of day". The important thing is to do it!

There are many positions and types of Meditative practice. I am not going to cast any aspersions that say one is the better or the best. They all strive to achieve the same result, they just use different approaches. Some use sound to cause certain vibrations, some use colors, others holding certain positions. All are good it is just the belief and viewpoint that changes.

Personally, I like to come home after a hard day at work and meditate to calm myself before bed. I go into my room and turn off the lights. I get comfortable in a chair and put some of my favorite music on. I close my eyes and take the tip of my tongue and gently place it on the roof of my mouth just behind my teeth. This helps to connect the Governing and Conception Vessel meridians. I breathe in through the nose allowing my abdomen to expand, (diaphragmatic breathing) and exhale through the mouth. Once I start I focus on taking in all the good energy with each breath and feeling all of the days stress and negative feelings going out with each exhale. As my body relaxes I just let it go. It finds its own rhythm and place. I'm in a place where the only thing that is, is me!

When I am finished I am so relaxed that some times it takes a while for me to be able to move. There is no more tension or stress, just peace! This is, after all, one of the many reasons that I started training. Over many years and after a few bumps and bruises I am starting to understand some of the things we are taught.

I remember on one occasion being told "We all make choices in life, and we have to live with the consequences of those choices!" This is so true.

Knowing that it is within your reach to improve your health, my question to you is: What is your Choice?

HEALTH

Also note that when we breathe we are not just taking in air, we are taking in the energy from the universe around us. This energy from the universe around us is an essential part of our being. It is this energy (chi) that couples with the energy within our body to sustain and nourish us. LIFE!

I have read that according to Chinese medical theories that the skin is regarded as a third lung. If this is true, then our skin is doing this also!

Has anyone ever had the sensation while meditating that feels like air coming and going everywhere? Your arms, legs, hands, everywhere! I know that I have and when I did it a very strange feeling. It felt like the air no longer was going in and out of my lungs. I could not feel them filling; and emptying though I "knew" that they had to! I'm not so sure anymore. All I do know for sure is, I didn't suffocate and when I was finished I was more relaxed and rested than ever before!

Our body and mind have the tools needed to heal and correct many of the health problems that attack us. Our job is to give it what it needs to do so! This brings us back to the beginning. Life is a cycle, high and low, light and dark, positive and negative. As in the Yin - Yang symbol, each has the seed of the other. Ever changing back and forth in a harmonious rhythm. Go with it! Feel the Power.

Chapter 10 - Mind Over Matter 127

Chapter 11

Rest and Motion

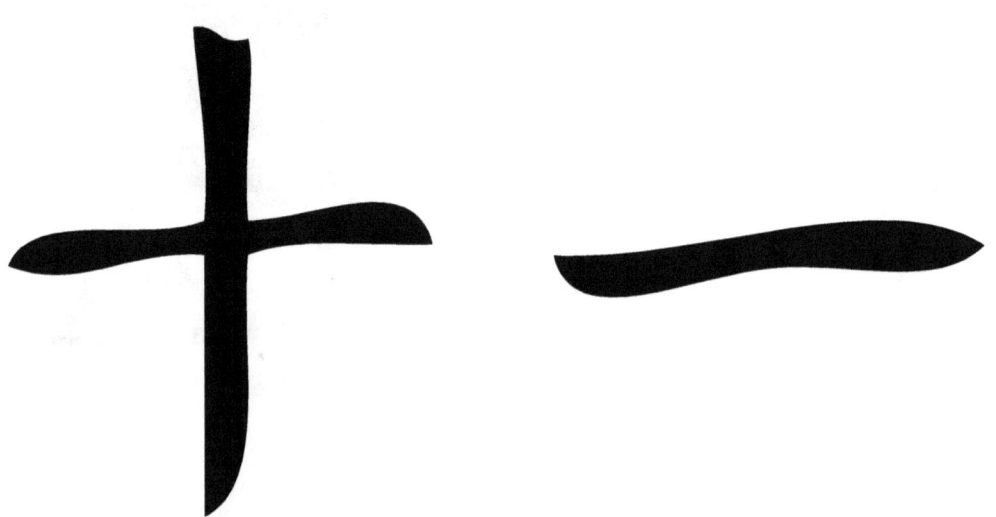

Chapter 11 - Rest and Motion

In our busy lives, there is no time to stop and simply reflect. Reflection, however, we need. The ability to reflect is what makes us human. Our minds are capable of taking ideas, experiences, events and extrapolating them to images and visions.

So much of our time right now is focused on fighting fires, addressing immediate concerns. As the image implies, putting out fires is a constant running around without giving yourself time to stop and grasp the situation. Adrenaline is put into constant overdrive and our bodies never have time to rest.

In today's world, this constant push has driven the business of curing mental issues to an all time high. Sleep deprivation, stress syndromes, constant and habitual use of medication; all have become a part of our daily worlds. And the number one advise that all the psycho-therapist and doctors give is the simplest prescription of all - meditation.

Meditation is the key to reflection. Meditation opens the door to the mind and awakens our "third-eye" to see "beyond the present and into the future."

Meditation is also more than just sitting in lotus position in isolation of all else, especially not your own body. The basic concept of meditation is to become one with yourself, to learn and understand oneself.

Meditation also doesn't imply one is practicing any given religion.

While many religions, both eastern and western, use forms of meditation as part of their practice, there isn't anything innately linking meditation to any set religion. In fact, if we were to derive the history of meditation, the true origins come from natural occurrences in our lives - moments of slumber and winters where there is nothing to do but rest.

Meditation at Rest

The first way most people learn to meditate is in a rested position - be that in a seated or lying posture. The lack of movement allows one to focus just on the basic of life - breathing. Meditation at rest frees the mind, allowing it to wander and open the third-eye chakra to the world around us.

The final objective is to clear the mind - relieving stress and tension.

However, it takes a great deal of time and patience to reach this state.

Many people, upon hearing the final state, attempt to rush the process, force themselves to think of nothing. All this accomplishes is to create tension and frustration - the exact opposite of the state they wish to create.

Just as in the internal arts in general, one must let "what energy that wishes to exist, exist." Allow yourself the freedom to let your thoughts flow and go where they please. Only when they have completed their course will one find peace and the clarity of mind that comes with meditation.

Begin by finding someplace quiet, where you can not be distracted for

Chapter 11 - Rest and Motion

a period of time. The period of time depends upon what you have and what your mind will allow you. It could be as short as fifteen minutes or last for a few hours. Set the mood as best you can, whatever relaxes you. If you find silence and darkness calming, then turn everything off. If you find more comfort in music, select music that has no words, nothing to distract you on a train of thought (because the art of speaking and hearing requires us to concentrate on physical things). If darkness distracts you, then just leave the lights dimmed until they no longer penetrate through your closed eyelids.

Get into a position that is most comfortable for you. For each of us that will be slightly different. For some, sitting long lengths of time is painful. For others, lying on their back can be annoying. Find the position that is most comfortable for you and don't be afraid to experience and try different things. There are many stationary postures located in the Tai Chi Postures manual that could be utilized.

Once you've found the right setting and the best position for you, you have found the optimal state to enter into meditation at rest. You have probably also just found the optimal situation to fall asleep. Try your best not to fall asleep but be aware of all that is happening to you - the way your chest rises and falls as you breathe, the weight or lightness of your arms and legs, the earth beneath you or the air moving against your skin. Then slowly let those things go, release those thoughts to roam as they will until there is emptiness and a true opening of the mind.

Meditation in Motion

True meditation is a state of being. Thus, it can be done at rest or in motion. Trying to reach a meditative state while in motion, however, is a lot harder. For most people, as they do a move or form, they think about the next motion or the target or a number of other physical things on top of what normally roams on people's minds. We are trained in Martial Arts to think this way, to try to read our opponent and anticipate their next move.

To meditate while in motion, one needs to bring the reflection close: to home, to internalize the thoughts. It becomes a matter of looking inside for where the next "attack" will come rather than from some external force The movement of the body simply allows for the thoughts to flow with them, like streams of blood and chi that run throughout.

Just as in meditation at rest, the third eye chakra is opened and one must let their thoughts flow to clarity to reach the ultimate state. It doesn't occur immediately, taking years to reach that state and master. For some, they may never reach this state.

As one practices to meditate in motion, it begins by familiarizing yourself with the movements. Understand how the body moves, why it moves. All movement is not just an isolated muscle, joint or bone. It is the whole body, in its entirety that drives all motion forward. Eventually, there is a point where the movements become so familiar that it requires little to no thought - only then can one begin to push towards meditation in motion.

When thoughts of the actual movements fall to the side, the mind will begin to wander on whatever worries fill you. Often times, this can cause you to miss a beat or forget a motion, pushing you back to the first state of conscious movement. Don't fight this stage, let the thoughts flow just as you would in seated meditation. Eventually with continued practice, these other thoughts lessen and quiet. And at one point, there will be total clarity of the mind and a true opening of the third-eye chakra.

While most of this is written in the context of your training, true meditation in motion doesn't have to just occur while just doing Martial Arts. It can happen during simple events, like walking down the street.

In fact, for many of us we do end up slipping into that state without realizing it. We focus on a problem or a situation in our lives with such intensity

Chapter 11 - Rest and Motion

that we might drive all the way home and not realize we were ever behind the wheel of our vehicles. And while this is reaching towards meditation in motion, one must be aware that this is actually one of the furthest points from that state.

When we get into a situation where thought takes over all of our conscious state, we forget about the oneness of our entire being. It is the oneness that makes meditation powerful.

Benefits of Meditation

Be it in motion or at rest, an internalist or externalist, we must all take the time to learn meditation. From a purely internal perspective, meditation helps us to heal ourselves. Stress is one of the major causes of most of our physical illnesses and one of the main things reduced by practicing meditation. Meditation helps us to focus our energy and builds awareness of our bodies and ourselves.

For an externalist, meditation is a powerful tool not only to prepare yourself for combat but during combat as well. When I think of meditation in the external arts, I often drum up the picture of Keanu Reeves in the Matrix as he stands there easily blocking each punch as if he were simply a spectator watching. By opening the third-eye chakra, one begins to understand more than just the next movement of their opponent, but to actually feel the flow of the battle.

As humans, we must all take the time to meditate. If for nothing else, we must take the time to reflect, to remember we are alive. To consider the very code which we have all chosen to live by: "I am what I am because I choose to be, a dragon by choice."

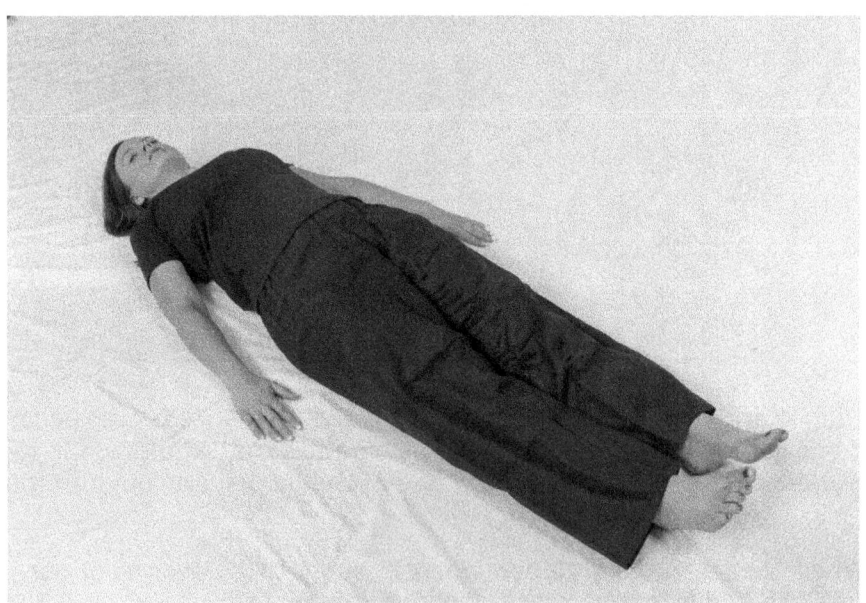

Chapter 11 - Rest and Motion

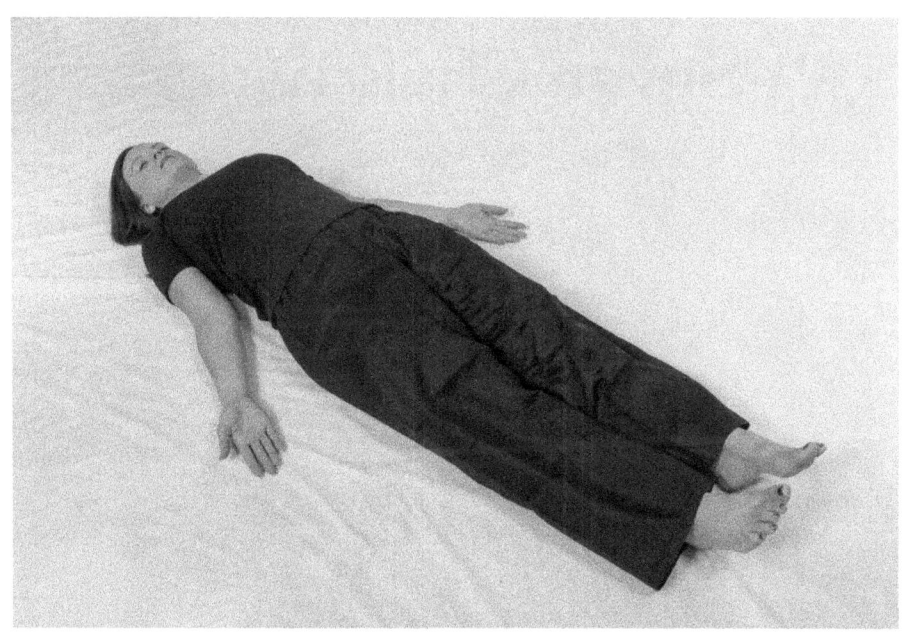

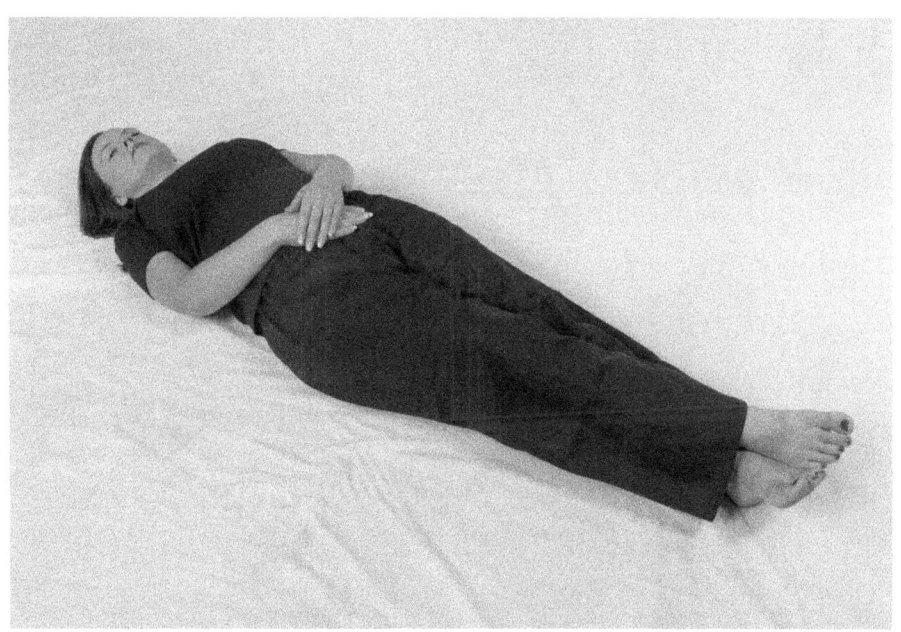

Chapter 12

Seven Chakras

Chapter 12 - Seven Chakras   137

Chakra One-"O"-Earth

You are beginning your beautiful journey.

It is a journey of your own layers of existence.

You are earth from which all grows, You are solid and alive.

You are at the foundation, a solid and tangible manifestation.

Your journey begins in the root of your own body, base of your spine

It begins now with wherever you are, your earth creation.

It is your own personal quest of self, your path on earth.

Your energy is awakened and motion begins, you feel a tremor.

You begin to move within, a virgin feeling of excitement.

Chakra Two-"OO"-Water

Your earth body remains still, yet you feel movement within.

The ever existing flow of water - your internal river.

The endless flow of breath, pushing the river.

A constant balance of waves against the shore.

A rhythm of life - heart beating moisture through streams of life.

Your waterfall crashing harmonious rhythms of energy.

Your belly sways a warm energy flow through your genitals, your life, your sex.

You feel the ocean vast and deep, abound with life.

You are water, the essence of all forms, yet formless.

Chakra Three-" AH"-Fire

With each breath we ignite a spark of fire, of warmth.

Our blood flows through our body as lava from a volcano.

We call upon our Self to awaken to the warmth of transformation.

The flames will burn within us and temper our passions into strength.

We feel the fires of life evoke our joy and anger within, Accept it.

The warmth and fire of others is all around us. Share.

Filaments of energy shoot pulsating beams effortlessly through you.

Your power peaks and returns in an endless change.

Fires burn high, coals are glowing, you are exhilarated.

Chakra Four-"AY"-Air

Bathing in air, wisping along your skin, through your hair, in your lungs, renewing you.

Hear your own heart, as a rhythm, beating life ever-changing.

You feel the balance of giving and receiving compassion, love, fulfillment.

With every heartbeat, inhale. You will feel yearning, crying, loving, hoping, healing.

You listen deep within, hear the silent sound.

Touch with your hands, yet you feel with your heart.

We reach out and spread our wings and ride the wind like a dragon.

Here lies the lotus of the celestial wishing tree.

You have found the center of love, as spirit and water are combined.

Chakra Five-"EE"-Sound

Breathe deeply, Feel your thoughts expand, listen to the still path.

Create your vibration and recognize yourself.

Chant inside quietly, rising up from deep within, feel your Rhythms pounding.

Communicate with your creativity and feel the connection of "I".

Create your mantras, hear the travel through your body.

Hear the spirit of the dragon stir in your neck, shoulders, arms, hands.

Your sound vibration is your self-expression, it controls, creates, transmits, and receives.

Our sounds unite us in our journey, harmonizing, purifying the profound TRUTH.

Our sound chakra sends us through space, beyond our previous four elements.

Chakra Six-"MMM" or "NNN"-Light

It is dark, yet we can still see, beloved third eye ~ light of all.

Through our chakra we feel our mind expand, endless images of truth.

Through shapes and images insight is revealed, nothing remains concealed.

When thine eye becomes single, one's body shall be filled with intuition and visual perception.

Our Light is a key to our energy, for its speed is a timeless wave entering us.

Through our third eye wavelengths of light relay colors through which perceive the light.

The light of visualizations, we see not with our eyes, it is purely the soul.

One realm of visual ~ direct perception, memory, imagination, precognition, dreams.

Step out of the middle of your being, learn to truly see, see the center and aura.

Chakra Seven-"NG"- Thought

Through one's crown we find the wisdom within, there is nothing beyond.

The keys we hold within our mind, the answer to all is within our keys.

Within this chakra we find our knowledge, bliss and understanding of "I BE."

Our thoughts, no form, endless sound, colorless light, empty space, ever flowing time.

Through the passage of our crown, we find the gateway to worlds beyond.

Our crown is the directional message to free our other chakras.

Nothing in our life is stagnant, least of all our perfection, this will enlighten us.

The thousand petals of our Lotus unfolds wisdom and understanding a thousand fold.

Chapter 12 - Seven Chakras

We have come full circle, our journey is complete and begins the endless sea of infinity.

Chakra	One	Two	Three
Element	Earth	Water	Fire
Energy State	Solid	Liquid	Blood
Psychological	Survival	Desire	Will
Results	Grounding	Sexuality	Power
Emotion	Stillness	Tears	Joy & Anger
Color	Red	Orange	Yellow
Foods	Proteins	Liquids	Starches
Body Parts	Large Intestines	Kidney, Bladder	Digestive
Sounds	O As in Rope	OO As in Due	AH As in Father

Chakra	Four	Five
Element	Air	Sound
Energy State	Gas	Vibration
Psychological	Love	Communication
Results	Balance	Creativity
Emotion	Compassion	Connection
Color	Green	Blue
Foods	Vegetables	Fruits
Body Parts	Lung, Heart	Throat, Mouth
Sounds	Ay As in Pray	EE As in Free

Chapter 12 - Seven Chakras

Chakra	Six	Seven
Element	Light	Thought
Energy State	Image	Information
Psychological	Intuition	Understanding
Results	Imagination	Knowledge
Emotion	Dreaming	Bliss
Color	Indigo	Violet
Foods	Fasting	Fasting
Body Parts	Eyes	Fasting
Sounds	MMM, NNN	NG As in Sing

Meditation is one of the best methods to safely develop your internal power. The purpose of this article is to give you a clear understanding of where your state of mind needs to be as you meditate. Also, it will provide you with the overall understanding of what lies within you for your journey to develop the powerful force within you.

Energy is all around you. The ability to accept it and become acquainted with it is key to meditation. This energy affects the body, mind and spirit. Kirlian photography has been able to show that an energy field surrounds every living thing. There are also some basic drills you can do which will allow you to experience your own energy. One way to do this is to open and close both your hands several times. Then, move the palms of both your hands towards each other (starting from a distance). As your palms get closer to each other you should be able to feel a tingling sensation or even a sense of slight resistance between your palms. The distance between your palms will vary depending on the amount of energy being emitted from your hands. If the energy is strong, you may be able to feel the energy while your hands are 6 inches or more apart. Or, you may need to have your palms nearly touching to feel the sensation. It doesn't matter how far apart your palms are from each other as long as they aren't physically touching each other since that would defeat the purpose of sensing the energy fields between your palms as they intercept. You can also work this with a partner, which will allow you experience the difference between your energy and theirs. Now that you've experienced your own energy, it's of importance to realize that this energy field is affected by our physical and emotional states, so your thoughts, actions and attitudes positively or negatively affect your energy.

Your energy field is made up of chakras. Chakras are recognized across many cultures but are most closely linked to the practice of yoga. A chakra refers to any of the seven energy centers within the body. The chakras correspond to various items, such as color, sound, element, food type, etc. In order to gain a clearer understanding of the chakras within the body (as it applies to developing your internal power), you must have an idea of how they look and where they're located. Imagine a stacked column of seven "plates" or "wheels of light" within the core (or along the body's spine). In order for you to visualize this in your body, imagine the plate positioned at a corresponding location within the body as follows:

Chapter 12 - Seven Chakras

Chakra	Location	Sound	Color
Seven	Top of the head	Ng (sing)	Violet
Six	Center of the forehead	Mmmmm	Indigo
Five	Throat	Ee (Sleep)	Blue
Four	Heart	Ay (Play)	Green
Three	Solar Plexus	Ah (Father)	Yellow
Two	Lower Abdomen (Tan Tien)	00 (Dew)	Orange
One	Base of Spine	"Oh" (Rope)	Red

The above picture depicts a model of the chakras along with the energy flowing through the chakras.

Now that you have a clearer picture of the chakras as they relate to your own body and energy field, you must also imagine the energy flowing through this column of chakras. Since energy requires both the positive and negative current, each chakra serves as the intersection point of this positive and negative flow of current, resulting in a major energy source corresponding to each chakra location. Visualizing this, you can also think of each chakra as a "battery" located with your body.

The energy within your body is emitted via each chakra as well as the energy, which flows up and down this central column, resulting in the source of your aura or energy field. Although some can see this aura as color(s) or as a vague source of opaque light, the most important point is to understand that you have this tremendous energy system and the capability to nurture it.

The chakras exist in various states such as open, closed, excessive or deficient, yet they are intertwined with each other, which, together, make up your energy system within your body. The chakras are only separated by concept to gain a better understanding of their location and purpose within your body.

Through appropriate meditation techniques, such as sound vibrations or visualization techniques, you have the ability to open all seven of your chakras and unleash the powerful force within you. However, if you expect to put a timetable of a few days or weeks to develop this force within, you would be overly self-confident. The most productive approach is a balanced, gradual effort, like the gentle, continual flow of water. Perseverance and patience are the keys as you enjoy your journey. If you are true to yourself and are able to "tune in" to your own energy, you can develop your own power because it exists in all of us. Our energy system is yet another thing that makes each of us unique like our fingerprints or personalities. Energy systems have distinctive qualities and attributes, no one is better than the other, they are just different.

Once you've developed your internal power, you can harness it with your will or intent to develop the capacity for amazing feats! Although working with your chakras will certainly enhance your martial arts training, whether it's Tai Chi, Kung Fu, Kenpo or SanShou, it also permeates throughout all activities and interactions in your life. Through the knowledge of this system you can positively impact your life in nearly unlimited ways. Some of the ways it can help you are:

Increase power and energy

Increase awareness or receptiveness to compassion

Develop intuition

Increase perception

Combining Pai Lum Tao's meditation tools and techniques along with the knowledge of your energy system, you have the ability to develop your internal power through your positive thoughts, emotions and actions, resulting in a healthy mind, body and spirit.

Chapter 12 - Seven Chakras

Chapter 13

Teenagers and Meditation

Chapter 13 - Teenagers and Meditation

There are many approaches to meditation, but the generally agreed purpose is to train the mind to observe, and to then let go of attachments in order to simply be "mindful". Whatever the method, after one begins to quiet the mind, one's life becomes more peaceful. The mindfulness one gets through the practice of meditation will be carried on in their daily activities and life. When the mind settles down, it lets go of tension and stress. Through proper meditation we

can find happiness; those times when we set ourselves free from regrets about the past or anxiety about the future. Teenagers are often challenged with these feelings. They are experiencing a life changing stage of being.

Today, more and more teenagers are visiting psychologists, psychiatrists and seeking help from counselors. This has become much too common in middle schools as well as high schools throughout the western world. Stressful factors such as a challenged education system, student competition, peer pressure, parental pressures, common teenage issues and demanding expectations from our friends are taking their toll on teenagers today. Peer pressure today is at an all time high for our youth. They are on a fast track to high levels of stress and

anxiety that have never been seen before.

Teenagers must learn to accept themselves and other people, handle tough situations in life, make themselves responsible and efficient and learn to tackle feelings like depression. Lack of confidence, loneliness and poor concentration

Chapter 13 - Teenagers and Meditation

are also challenges they must face daily. Through Chin Kon Pai meditation, good relationships, proper guidance, a positive attitude and outlook, along with a lot of laughter, teens are encouraged to tackle various issues and challenges.

Many feel that all teenagers should practice meditation and create an effective training program for themselves that empowers them to be more centered and balanced. They must learn to experience calmness and inner clarity while meeting every day's obstacles. Through a regularly practiced meditation training teens will master a breathing process that can permanently reduce stress and heighten one's mental clarity and awareness. Practiced on a regular basis it will improve concentration, enhance creativity, increase efficiency and productivity and enable a greater sense of our belonging. This can also serve to create new relationships and friendships in a positive and caring environment.

Teenagers are faced with so many changes in their mind and body. It becomes confusing at times and they would benefit greatly from the positive benefits of proper training and guidance. It would give them a greater sense of value as well as a stronger relationship with those that truly care for them such as family. All teenagers should be encouraged to practice meditation to help find a center and peace in their life.

The youth of today are longing for guidance and direction. In an age of instant gratitude and life in the fast lane, some centered exercise of mind based skills is truly what is needed. Sometimes one just needs to slow things down and think clearly about what is really happening around them. One day they feel like an adult and the next day they seem childlike. These are common emotions that they may struggle with for years.

During a very vulnerable time in their life, clarity is very important to help in decision making. Decisions made now can and often will affect them the rest of their lives. Any tool that is a positive one should be utilized to assist during these adolescent years. Meditation is an exercise that they can practice in private or within a group of their peers. This too adds to the strength of the gathering with a good purpose.

Meditation can serve to bond parents and their children by practicing together on a regular basis. A new found respect and tolerance can be formed through this type of union. A new attitude may emerge that is coupled with friendly demeanors and smiling faces. That is something that will warm the hearts of all parents.

With all the changes going on within teenagers during their challenging years, physical and mental health is a great concern. A greater enhanced health for them is much more likely when they slow their bodies and minds down to understand inner peace and tranquility. They will assist greatly in ridding or reducing stress, anxiety and unease. This will help in their natural growth, immune system and all of their natural functions. It will help them achieve what all parents want for their children, love and light coupled with peace and joy.

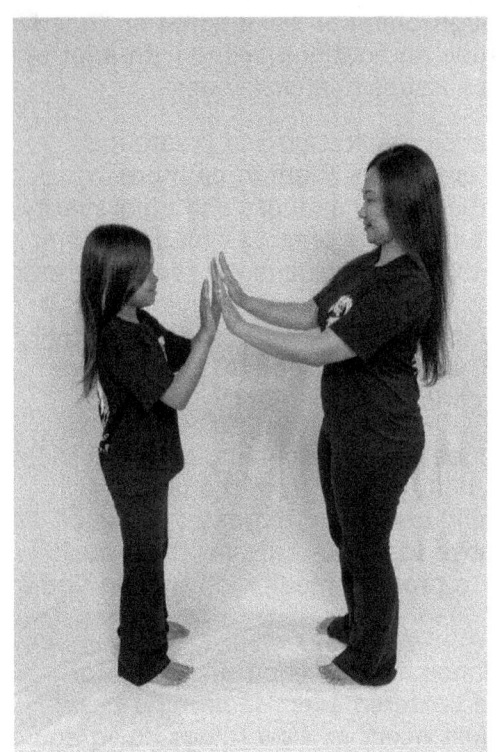
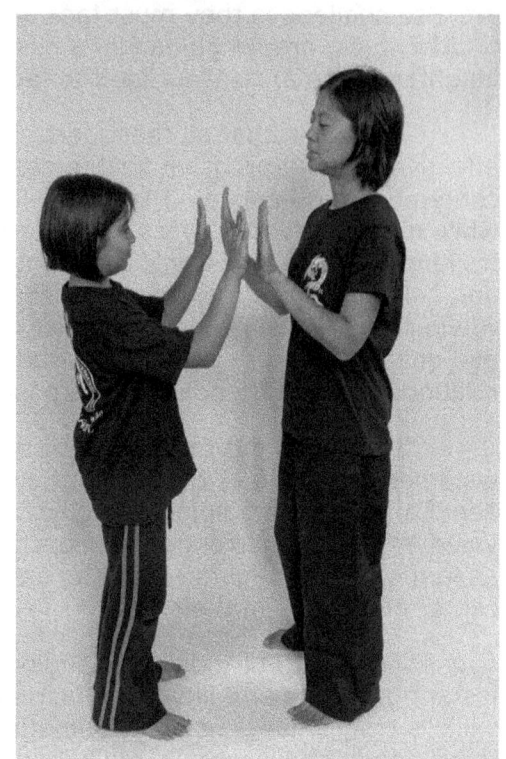

Chapter 13 - Teenagers and Meditation

Chapter 14

Guided Meditation

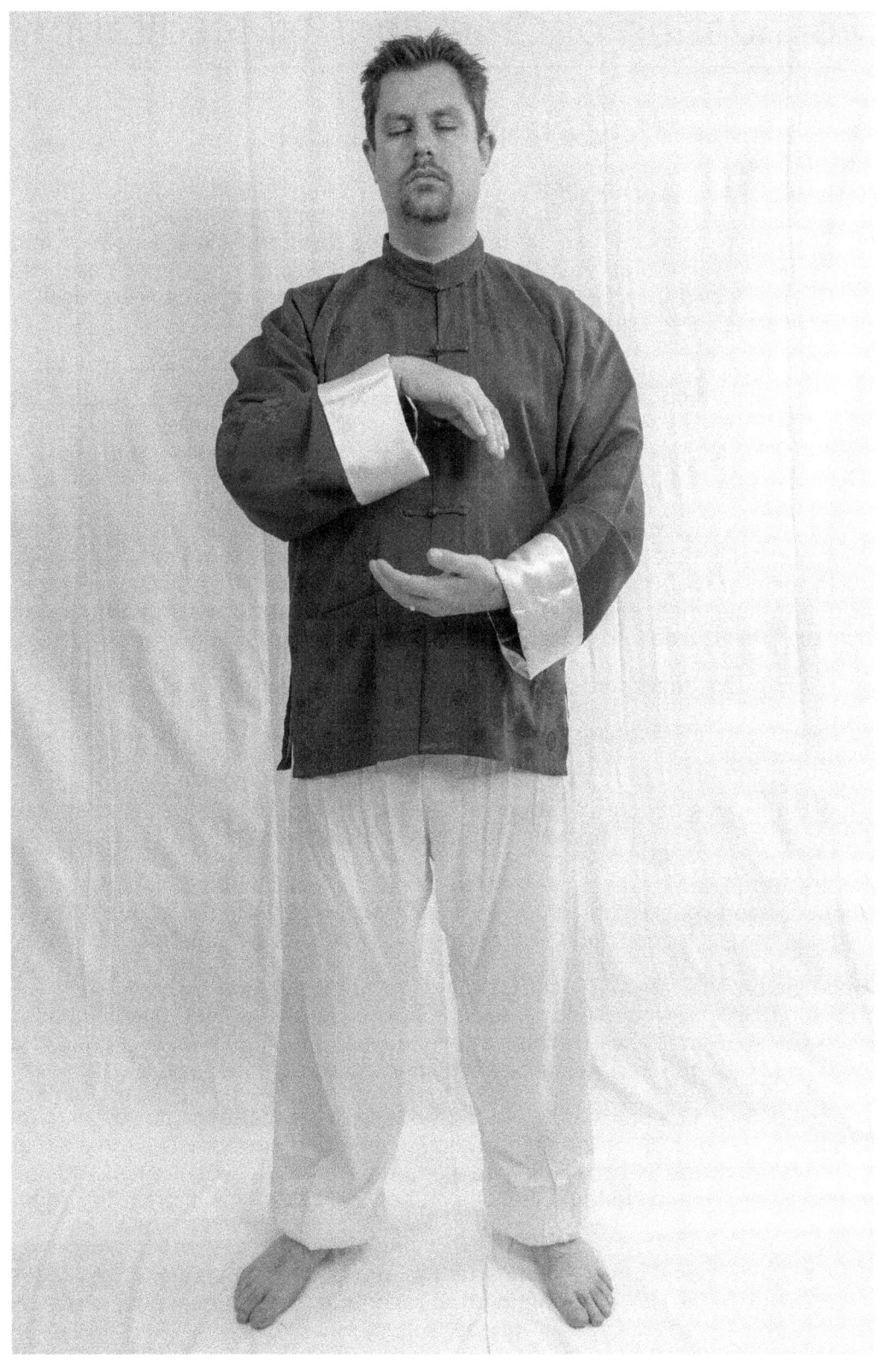

Foundation of Chin Kon Pai Meditation

Zen Meditation

Zen meditation is the practice of sitting in grounding and calming your body, mind and spirit opening yourself up to understanding who you are deep inside. As you 'the practitioner' sit in your desired position, you secure your mind to distracting thought then your breathing will slow down to a tranquil pace, the heart rate will slow down yet still be strong, you will pass into a philosophical meditative state of thought & thinking.

When you are practicing Zen Meditation, your thoughts will be focusing in the moment. That is the moment that you now reside and exist in. You should not be contemplating your past or the future. At this time you should be thinking thoughts of healing, peace, the beauty within you and surrounding you. These thoughts become fuel for your future action and decisions.

You are concentrating on the moment at hand only. Your thought becomes specific and deliberant on what we call 'The Now'. There is always thought taking place in some part of the mind. To subdue it from distraction and concentrate in a peaceful, tranquil manner on only 'The Now' all challenges of past and future are minimized. This is true Zen as taught in Chin Kon Pai Meditation.

Some very important steps to your practice of Zen meditation are:

Recognize your breathing patterns. Know them as your 'inhale and exhale' patterns.

Follow the rhythm of your breathing and recognize the difference between 'deep breathe and shallow breathe'.

With your inhale you must concentrate on your physical body and strength of muscle, upon your exhale you will totally relax all parts of the body. This will begin in the neck and shoulder area then work downward one area at a time.

Upon your inhale you will focus on calming the muscle and body parts. When you begin to exhale you need to visualize the nutrients and feed the 'compassion thought' to your entire being. This not only is good meditation it has been proven to be a form of self healing and centering one's self.

Once the body is in a state of relaxation you should concentrate on relaxing your facial muscles one at a time. All that is happening in our body is expressed in our facial muscles. By consciously relaxing the entire face we are sending and confirming peace and tranquility to the rest of our body. This is great for ridding ourselves of poisoning stress.

Take a mental travel of your body attempting to find any tense or stress-laden areas. Then use the power of the mind to relax that area and cast out any stress or challenges.

With every inhale you will think of peace, joy, life, happiness, power of being one with your self.

Return to your mental state of recognizing your breathing patterns. You have made a complete cycle of self.

Chakra Meditation

Chakra meditation is utilized to balance and channel in good energy and to get rid of negative energy that accumulates in your body. The seven major and thousands of minor chakras found within our body are the centers for energy within the body. The practice of chakra meditation will keep our energy balanced and in proper alignment.

Chakra meditation can be practiced in several different positions including standing, seated in a chair, floor seated postures and lying down. You can choose which ever one you are most comfortable in at the moment or keep it as a regular practice posture for your sessions. The most important thing is that you are relaxed and comfortable to unsure easier chi flow through the chakras.

The beginning preparation for chakra meditation is very important.

Choose a quite, peaceful, uninterrupted location.

Wear loose fitting comfortable clothing.

Choose your meditation position.

Do not have an overly full or empty stomach.

If you choose a tranquil music, play it softly in the background.

If you choose a mellowing sent, light your incense or candle.

Align your head and back in a natural relaxing state to assure the chakras are open.

Begin your thought process to focus on the chakra of choice.

Your thought, reflection & contemplation will bring about a rumination and balance of energy.

Chakra meditation is varied in purpose and targeting thought for specific results.

Chakra meditation is very powerful and should be completed after about thirty to forty five minutes.

When choosing the practice of chakra meditation it is important to be educated in the intricacies of the seven chakras. A full understanding of their effect on the mind, body and health of ones self is mandatory before beginning. The first chakra that one should make healthy and strong is the root chakra known a number one major chakra.

Chakra number two is the naval chakra. This chakra is located around the womb or naval and is the stimulus for sexual pleasure, creativity and bliss.

The third chakra is known as the solar plexus chakra. It is located in the solar plexus area. The solar plexis chakra controls restraint, power and self-discipline.

In chakra meditation, the fourth chakra is one that we know oh so well, it is known as the heart chakra. The heart chakra is our center system famous for feelings, love and heart break. Most of our emotions are cultivated and come from this chakra.

The fifth chakra is known as the throat chakra. This very important chakra is located at the throat and is the center for our communication. It is believed that our wisdom and honesty are cultivated in the throat chakra. Since communication is the key ingredient in the formula for good relationships, chakra five is invaluable.

The next chakra that is contemplated during chakra meditation is the sixth chakra. It is known in Chin Kon Pai meditation as the all seeing third eye chakra. This important chakra is located directly between our eyes. Perception, insight, clairvoyance, thought, instinct, intuition and imagination are all credited to this marvelous chakra.

Our seventh chakra is known as the crown chakra, it is associated with our spirit and mind. Manifestation of the thoughts and visions within our mind are attributed to this highest chakra. Cogitation of one's spirit and strength of mind is affected by this chakra.

Guided Meditation

With guided meditation your thoughts are escorted on a journey. You are assisted by another's voice and message. One's ultimate purpose is to achieve a realization through fixed reflection and manifestation. There are a few different ways to achieve and receive the guided message. Someone may read or speak a guided thought to you in person, listen to a trainer on a CD, have a message played on a television, or record your own message and play it back at the time of your guided session. The purpose is to clear the mind of clutter and concentrate on the message that you are hearing, thus allowing your subconscious mind to follow the words that are being spoken to you. Even if you doze off or eventually fall asleep you will continue to hear and process the message subconsciously.

An effortless guided meditation will assist you to achieve relaxation. One will find that they have released much unwelcome negativity and emotions that

Chapter 14 - Guided Meditation

will hamper our spiritual growth. When you enter into a peaceful / comfortable relaxation you can feel feelings that are frequently buried in remote parts of your mind. When you allow your conscious mind to slumber, experiences are directed forward and are acknowledged by your subconscious mind. This is known as an 'awakening exercise.' It is very important that one practicing guided meditation maintain a positive and trusting state of mind. Your present and past experiences should be viewed in a positive light, you must learn from them all. Positive contemplation and reflection can also replace negative brainwashing with a strong and powerful confidence and high self esteem. This is not only a gift to you yourself it is beneficial to all of those that you come in contact with.

A Chin Kon Pai Guided Meditation practice is as follows:

Find a comfortable sitting position.

Bend your head slightly forward.

Close your eyes.

Place your hands in a chosen comfortable position.

Make sure your back is straight.

Be sure your entire body is relaxed, including your facial muscles.

Breathe in your nose and out through your mouth.

Gently touch your tongue to the roof of your mouth.

Slow your breathing down.

Feel the rhythm of your breath and heat.

Inhale with a deep breath then hold for a count of nine.

Exhale to the count of nine.

This exercise will continue for about thirty seconds.

On your last inhale, hold the breathe for a nine count, and then exhale.

For about thirty seconds maintain a shallow/slow breathing pattern.

Repeat the previous deep breather exercise for about thirty seconds.

After the second session of deep breathing repeat the shallow breathe.

Envision your body becoming lighter and your body rising up.

Visualize a white light surrounding your body and entering your being.

Imagine the white light consuming all of your negativity, anger, pain, fear and sickness.

Imagine the white light turns a shining gold and expels all of the above mentioned.

You experience a glowing, warm, beautiful, comforting sensation deep in your core.

Sit in the middle of the magnificent gold light and feel your breath feeding your body.

Inhale a shallow breath and wiggle your fingers and toes.

Continue your shallow breath and wiggle your ankles, wrist then legs, arms.

Maintain shallow breath and lift your head straight up very slowly.

Slowly open your eyes and take in all that you see.

You have journeyed with the voice of the one guiding you through your own path and discovery. This has now helped you in your own healing and spiritual grown.

Advanced Level Chin Kon Pai Exercises

An introductory advanced level exercise practiced within Chin Kon Pai meditation is done as follows:

Sit in a comfortable position with your hands on your knees or placed on top of each other covering your Tan Tien.

Extend your lower back and spine, hold your head upward and straight, relax your shoulders yet do not drop them.

Lower your eye lids yet do not close them all the way. Gaze softly at the inside of your eye lids.

Chapter 14 - Guided Meditation

Inhale slowly and deeply (over a period of 7 seconds) through your nose.

Visualize your breath moving from your chest down into your Tan Tien (a point just below the naval) and hold it there for 7 seconds.

Exhale out your mouth for about 7 seconds, listen to the sound and rhythm of your breathe.

Bind together the energy from heaven and from the earth. Visualize your energy moving circularly and continuously around your body while it fills entirely.

For males, visualize the movement of your energy from your third eye, down the front of your body to your Tan Tien then up the spine of your back to the forehead.

For females, visualize the movement of your energy from your third eye, down your back to a point midway between your forehead and Tan Tien then up your front to the forehead.

You should begin to feel your body temperature rise slightly. Sometimes one may feel a little itchy sensation due to energy transfer and body warmth. This is OK and will subside.

During this exercise it is very important to concentrate your thoughts and attention on the sound of your breathing.

This next advanced Chin Kon Pai meditation exercise should be practiced by students of one year or longer. Before beginning this exercise you should cleanse your mind. Think clear and good thoughts, pray to your lord for a heightened experience.

Sit with your legs outward (butterfly style), then join them at the soles, your knees will be relaxed and slightly raised.

Inhale slowly through your nose, hold your breath for a short period of time, slowly and silently exhale trough the mouth.

Join your hands together in prayer hand position, held in front of your heart.

Lean your upper body to the left side, your nose should always stay in line with your hands.

Repeat this motion to your right side.

Do the same motion forward, then backward. Be sure that your lower body remains still. Your center balance should be in your belly area. Keep your body relaxed yet firm.

You should do a total of three of the se series.

During these exercises you will chant the "Say E Tay" series. All of these chants must be learned directly from a certified Pai Lum Tao teacher.

Our third Chin Kon Pai meditation exercise is called the Immortal Man and should be practiced in the seated seiza stance.

Prepare yourself by relaxing your body and sit in seiza stance with your spine straight. The seiza stance is common to the Japanese / Zen influence of the arts. You will sit on your legs and feet while your big toes cross each other behind you. If you have discomfort in this stance start out by utilizing a pillow under you.

Join your hands together in front of your face while extending your index fingers outward and pointing to heaven. With males your right thumb should cover your left thumb and with females your left thumb should cover your right thumb.

Inhale through the nose, this should be done very slowly and deeply. As soon as you are full of fresh cleansing air you will begin your slow exhale through the mouth. A time reference should be three sets at 12 seconds, three seconds at 20 seconds and three sets at 30 seconds.

During this exercise you will visualize the heavens above you and the cleaning air of life passing deep into your body. This air is stirring your peaceful and passionate emotions for our wonderful existence.

As you become better at this exercise you will repeat this entire sequence twice and finally three time total.

Be sure that your body remains erect and stays relaxed. If your hands become too heavy and uncomfortable, place them on your lap and continue your exercise.

Chapter 14 - Guided Meditation
Say E Tay Chanting Meditation

This traditional chanting meditation has been guarded in the Pai Lum Tao system for many years. It was taught to students directly by Great Grandmaster Dr. Daniel Kalimaahaae Kane Pai during his journey on earth. It has been revered as a special chant for Pai Lum Tao members and only recently has been given openly to the world via internet. This was never Dr. Pai's wish. He wanted it to be taught correctly by a qualified instructor who trained directly with him. But alas, we are living in times of instant gratitude and a low level of respect for the traditional arts.

There are certain rhythms and pitches to the chant that will help the student reach a higher level of development in their journey of peace and power. Please check with a certified Pai Lum Tao teacher for proper guidance.

The Pai Lum Tao instructor will chant the following.

The class will echo the chant in harmony and with a peaceful state of mind.

The chants are done in a series of three each.

Say E Tay

Do E Ray

Fa E La

Peace and joy

We wish you

For ever more

This entire series is repeated a total of three times in harmony and at the pace set by the teacher / leader of the meditation chanting series.

Chapter 15

Peace and Joy

Peace & Joy Through Meditation

No matter where we live, what our cultural, ethnic, religious or social background is, most all of mankind seeks peace and joy in their daily lives. Some come closer to their desire of living a tranquil, non stressful life than others. There are many reasons for this variation in success for peace. We find throughout our experiences with many people seeking tranquility that they don't know how to relax their minds much less their bodies or vice versa.

It is impossible to be stressful, fearful, be anxious, hate or worry when your mind is focused on the opposite emotions aforementioned. We must choose what we want to contemplate on, we do not have to focus and concentrate on every thought that pops into your head, let the unwanted thoughts go.

The contents of your mind may be categorized in basic patterns; angry thoughts, frightened thoughts, resentful thoughts, desiring thoughts, planning thoughts, willing thoughts, happy thoughts, pleasurable thoughts, joyful thoughts and so on...

Your thought and the reaction to those thoughts are established over a lifetime of events. You will act or react a certain way due to the thoughts that you carry and how they relate to your memory of what is going on or possibly could take place very soon. Once you become aware of this and can work with it to establish and maintain a more restful state of mind, habitual patterns will lose their power over you. This is something we all should strive for.

Emotions trigger sensations in your body thousands of times a day. We must strive to manage these sensations by concentrating on them as opposed to the content of the thought. These sensations, emotions, thoughts and feelings are not permanent, let them pass through and give attention to what is good for you and desired.

Life becomes clearer and more manageable when you are aware and in tune with what is happening in the 'immediate' and you understand 'what is.' Your emotional rollercoaster of highs and lows will dissipate and life will become much more pleasurable and joyful.

Through the regular practice of meditation you will have a greater control of the thoughts and emotions that can cause us stress, anxiety and illness. Research and studies at some times can make the process complicated yet it really is basic to our nature. What are our very basic responses to meditation? Our breathing patterns will slow down to a comfortable rate, our heartbeat will in turn slow down releasing our treasured muscle from straining, oxygen consumption decreases by about twenty percent, blood lactate levels eventually drop (that helps rid us of stress), your epidermis is more resistant to currents and you will experience increased alpha activity in your brain. Wow, why wouldn't anyone want to meditate?

Through the practice of meditation you will find a greater and lasting peaceful nature within you. This will through continuous practice become a staple of who you are and what you give out to others around you. Your levels of relaxation will deepen and become longer lasting. Your attention to all around you becomes clearer and steadier. The present becomes much more comfortable and you will experience a steady level of peace and joy in your daily life.

What is most important is that we all walk our own path and seek our peace and joy in every day of our lives. Through meditation, healthy diet, good thought process, regular activity, wholesome relationships and faith in who we are and the greater power that helps guide us to the path of enlightenment, we will be one with that which is around us.

Begin your journey as you did with life itself, start off with baby steps and then forge yourself forward and never look back. Wish peace and joy for yourself so that you may give the gift to others.

Asian Healing – Western Healing

Even in our modern society and times that sharing of knowledge worldwide are not uncommon, Asian and Western philosophies and healing arts do differ. Western societies are geared towards the instant fix or more than likely masking of the ailment, unhappiness or disease. Take a pill, take photos of our deepest places within us, or so we think. Tell me your problems and now you are cured, does this happen much too often? This is truly not criticism or belittling ones beliefs, it is an effort to compare two very different views and schools of thought.

Within our 'law of the universe' we know there is always a cause and effect for all that is. We know this as karma, it is our own and we own it, good or bad, wanted or unwanted. So we know to find the root we must understand the cause, good or bad there is always a cause. If we do not identify and change the cause how can we expect to change our course and live a more satisfying existence? In the western world many choose to take a pill or many, many pills. Then if that does not work, cut it out; remove our ailment, leaving the cause still in existence. The cause has been ignored or missed.

The Asian philosophy and teaching is to identify and deal with the cause, not to be blinded by the symptom. First find out why a person is feeling what they feel and look for an alternative life practice to eliminate the cause. Certainly there is meditation and power of the mind, diet, sleep practices, herbs, acupuncture, acupressure and massage that a patient may partake in as a start. It must be a journey of patient and teacher that is safe, less expensive and not addictive. This works successfully for many people, it really is about an individual's choice. We do not profess what is right or wrong, it is about you and your individual process towards peace, joy and health.

A good and moderate philosophy has proven to be beneficial for many seeking the middle path and a healthier mind, body and spirit of existence. A few areas of concentration are:

Diet: Our unrest and disease are caused directly by the food we eat. How can anyone deny that you are what you eat? When we put food that is packed with chemicals, coloring, bacteria, preservatives and so on, our body finds itself in a state of non easiness which equals disease! Bad intake will certainly turn to poor performance and a killing of the internal parts.

Life Style: When we seek too much we seek to be unbalanced by nature. In western societies we strive to have, have, and have as much as possible with the belief that this will ensure us happiness. More than one will need becomes one's complications and mental illness. Do not forget or overlook the law of cause and effect, we can not bypass this ancient law. Learn to minimize and simplify one's lifestyle thus allowing the natural flow of things to exist within us. Unbalanced life style will surely equate to sickness, anxiety, dysfunctional attitudes and stress, this is the biggest killer of mankind in western societies.

Outlook: Being healthy and content begins with a positive attitude towards our daily life, those around us and ourselves. You cannot make an effect on your health and happiness without interjecting and practicing a optimistic and encouraging attitude. If you are negative most of the time, negativity will be attracted to your being. Your view point will be in a state of disorder and confusion much of the time. You will damage the immune system which must be kept in a positive state and in good working order, this really is natural not exceptional. One's body, mind and spirit are truly three dimensions of the same existing being. They must work well together and be subjected to positive and comforting fuel.

Spirituality: We understand that in modern times and societies that we must have some possessions and strive for the best fit in today's world. But, we must caution ourselves not to be controlled by the need for material things. We should concentrate on the desire for a higher state of spiritual development. It has never been proven that happiness comes from material objects. Values dependent on materialism is short lived and at most temporary. Suffering and discontentment come from the desire to have more and more of what we really need in moderation. Am I rich enough, do I know enough people, do I have a nice enough house, do I have enough money and am I good looking enough? At anytime during your growth in life you can answer your own question with 'yes'. Yes to all of the above because I have peace and joy in my life and my desires are simple yet fulfilling. I suffer none from the lack of anything, unless I choose to. I am the highest developed creature on God's earth, wow I am who I am because I choose to be.

Chapter 15 - Peace and Joy

Self healing is the key to our development and bliss. We certainly are influenced and assisted by those around us. Our family, our friends, our spiritual leaders, our teachers and our doctors/healers are a great influence of course. But in the end it is us, we do so alone!

We take life's breaths which influences our essential blood flow. Poor rhythms in the body will equate to poor blood flow which will eventually cause sickness to parts of the body or even death to our physical being. Blood is our energy pipeline and will have a profound influence on our every being of existence. Good blood flow to all parts of the body is key to good health of our skin and organs and even thought. Practices that are beneficial to good blood flow are Chi Kung exercise, Tai Chi Chuan movements, massage, warm bathing meditation, limited sun bathing, acupressure, acupuncture and herbs.

A key component to total health is proper breathing. This is something that we think we do naturally yet most people have very poor breathing habits. Proper breathing is most commonly thought of as breathing into our lungs and out of our body. We must remember that our skin breathes all the time and can be congested with chemicals that are put on it and the unnatural act of wearing clothing. We certainly understand that we must wear clothing to fit into social demands and that at time we feel that we must add cream or lotions to our skin, moderation in all practices can be very beneficial to our total health.

The practice of Chi Kung on a daily basis will be remarkable for anyone's health and existence. Breath exercises that are shallow and then deep will stimulate our organs and reach into our needed Tan Tien 'below the naval'. This area is known as the center of your being and stores and delivers our internal power when needed. The ancient saying is to breath like a baby. Let the oxygen travel deep and let the tummy expand with your breaths. This typically is done with a slow and deep inhale through the nose and a slow and patient exhale from the mouth. Best results are achieved when the exhale is longer than the inhale.

In our ever changing social existence as well as our ancient practices and philosophies one will find happiness and health through finding their own formula for peace and joy. It is an individual journey that all should partake in and spread as a positive message to all they meet. Not only in words but through a healthy action, this is much more likely to last and be more favorable to all.

My Teacher — Great Grandmaster Dr. Daniel Kalimaahaae Kane Pai

Grandmaster / Professor — Glenn C. Wilson

My Mentor — Shaolin Temple Lama Shi De Chao

We all wish for peace in our lives

We all have the power over our own destiny

We all are creatures of our creator's energy

We all are all powerful and enlightened

We all can spread peace and joy to those we encounter

We all posses the balance of yin and yang within us

We all are what we choose to be

Find Peace and Joy Through Daily Meditation

Chapter 16

Gallery

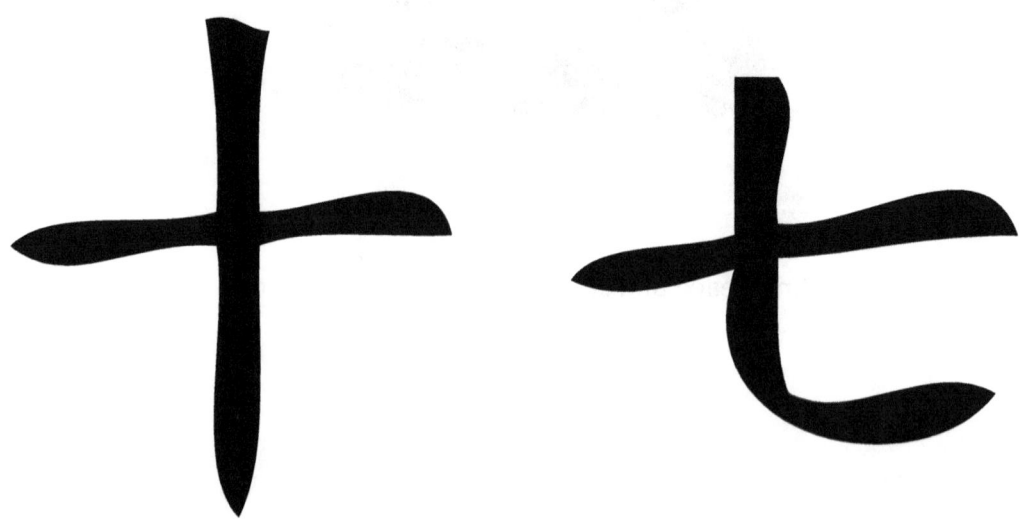

Chapter 16 - Gallery

Chapter 16 - Gallery

Chapter 16 - Gallery

Chapter 16 - Gallery

Chapter 16 - Gallery

Great Grandmaster Dr. Henry Seishiro Okazaki

Great Grandmaster Founder/Kaiso

So Doshin

Great Grandmaster Dr. Daniel Kalimaahaae Kane Pai

Lama Shi De Chao

Grandmaster Professor Glenn C. Wilson

Chapter 16 - Gallery

Be Sure to Collect the Rest of the "This Is Pai Lum Tao" Series

This is

Bok Leen Pai Kenpo

By Glenn C. Wilson

Grandmaster Glenn C. Wilson gives an in-depth look into the history and techniques of Bok Leen Pai Kenpo. Follow the development of this powerful, fascinating system as Grandmaster Wilson takes you from its birth in China, through Asia to Hawaii, and finally to the legendary Great Grandmaster Daniel Kalimaahaae Kane Pai as he brings Bok Leen Pai Kenpo and his Pai Lum Tao family of martial arts to the mainland of the United States.

With 16 chapters covering fist sets, forms, history, philosophy, five animal virtues, formulas and much more as well as 325 photos, some very rare, this book is a must-have for any serious student of the martial arts.

This is
Pai Lum Tao's Internal hand
By Glenn C. Wilson

Grandmaster Glenn C. Wilson brings to you the beauty and health aspects of this highly revered internal aspect of Pai Lum Tao Asian/martial arts. Savor the teachings of Great Grandmaster Dr. Daniel Kalimaahaae Kane Pai as you delve deeper into the internal arts of Asia. There are 207 pages of enlightenment and a journey through the internal arts of Pai Yung Tai Chi Chuan, Quan Nien Chi Kung and more.

Hundreds of photos will guide the reader through this peaceful voyage. There is detailed instruction and photos demonstrating the 'old style' Yang Short Form, Penetrate the Wind form and the rarely taught Quan Nien Buddhist Chi Kung Form series 1 through 6. This is certainly a very rare opportunity for any person to elevate their knowledge of the internal arts.

This is

Chin Kon Pai Meditation

By Glenn C. Wilson

This is the first book ever written on this most enchanting form of meditation, health and enlightenment. We learn of the history of meditation traveling from India to China to Japan and then eventually shared worldwide. Go deep into the psychology of meditation and what it really is. Understand the wide spread misconceptions of meditation and discover what it means to so many people throughout the world.

The reader will be guided through Chin Kon Pai meditation practice and discover the countless benefits to all. We truly are who we choose to be and through meditation we can discover the path to a beautiful journey of peace and joy as well as enhanced overall health. Find your own balance of mind, body and spirit. For centuries millions of people have felt the benefit of meditation now you can understand what Chin Kon Pai may do for you. This enlightening book has 200 pages with hundreds of photos to assist you on your journey's path.

This is
This is Pai Te Lung Kung Fu
By Glenn C. Wilson

Grandmaster Glenn C. Wilson helps you discover one of the most revered traditional styles of martial arts today. From the roots of Shaolin in China to its influences of travel through the Ryu Kyu islands, to it's modern development in Hawaii and its journey world wide. Pai Te Lung Kung Fu is respected as a powerful and extremely lethal system of Asian martial arts and forms of self defense.

The legendary Great Grandmaster Dr. Daniel Kalimaahaae Kane Pai developed a modern yet traditional art that was passed to him from some of the most learned minds of their time. He added his no nonsense way of life to assure a fighting art that is second to none. You will be introduced to the treasures of Pai martial arts such as, Iron Body, Nine creature fighting virtues, Philosophy, Healing, Wooden slide dummy, Traditional Forms, Combative fist sets, History, Photo gallery with rare photos and much more.

Explore 16 chapters, 225 pages and hundreds of photos on your journey into this most fascinating Asian art of combat, healing and philosophy.

Notes

Notes

Notes

剛軟拳法白龍道白蓮拳法

Notes

剛軟拳法白龍道白蓮拳法

Notes

Notes

www.ingramcontent.com/pod-product-compliance
Lightning Source LLC
Chambersburg PA
CBHW080543170426
43195CB00016B/2657